Living Well in a Down Economy For Dummies®

Cheat Sheet

W9-COW-261

Save on Energy Costs

The following tips, when combined together, can help cut your electricity and gas bills considerably:

- ✔ Find out whether your local energy provider has off-peak hours when electricity use is less expensive.
- ✔ Use a programmable thermostat that you can set for different temperatures at different hours.
- ✔ Wash clothes in cold water.
- ✔ If you need a cup or two of hot water, don't let the tap run until the hot water comes out; heat water in the microwave instead.
- ✔ If you have outdoor lighting for safety reasons, install motion detectors on the lights.
- ✔ Replace frequently used light bulbs with fluorescent bulbs.
- ✔ Refrigerators and freezers work better if they're full. Fill the empty spaces with clean milk jugs filled with water.
- ✔ Clean the coils of the fridge regularly so the cooling mechanism can run more efficiently.
- ✔ Use a water-heater insulation blanket and keep the water heater's temperature set at 120 degrees Fahrenheit.

Shop Smart

- ✔ Go to a "cash only" basis for budgeting.
- ✔ Shop from a list for everything from food to clothing to holiday gifts.
- ✔ Consolidate your little trips to the grocery store into one weekly trip to save on gas.
- ✔ Don't grocery shop when you're hungry. People who do usually spend more and buy more processed — and, therefore, more expensive — food.
- ✔ Buy merchandise when it's going out of season.
- ✔ Shop at discount stores, and buy dry goods in bulk.
- ✔ Avoid brand names when a generic equivalent is available.
- ✔ Don't buy impulsively.

For Dummies: Bestselling Book Series for Beginners

Living Well in a Down Economy For Dummies®

Cheat Sheet

Create a Budget in Three Easy Steps

Does the word *budget* send chills up your spine? It shouldn't. Budgets allow you to be organized and have some control over what you spend. They help you to decide how to spend your money, plan for your future, pay off existing debt, and save a few pennies each month by reducing wasteful and impulsive purchases.

1. **Categorize your expenses.**

   When you begin setting up a monthly budget, start with big categories before breaking your budget down into smaller expense categories.

   Within each general category, some items are essential (the mortgage or rent payment, the electric bill, and groceries), but other items are extra (new furniture, gifts, and pizza delivery). From your first list of general budget items, develop two separate budget lists, one for essentials and the other for extras.

2. **Estimate what you spend.**

   Go through your checkbook and any other receipts or records you've kept over the past few months so you can track how much you actually spend on essentials. Then for one month keep a detailed diary of all your extra purchases, even for cheap things like newspapers or coffee from the vending machine at work.

3. **Calculate and adjust.**

   To find out whether your spending habits are keeping you in the red, add up the essentials list and the extras list separately. Subtract the essentials total from your monthly income. If you have money left over, subtract the extras total from that amount. If your extras list takes you into negative numbers, start looking for places to cut back.

For Dummies: Bestselling Book Series for Beginners

Living Well in a Down Economy

FOR

DUMMIES®

Living Well in a Down Economy

FOR

DUMMIES®

by Tracy L. Barr

WILEY

Wiley Publishing, Inc.

(026427)

MAR 3 0 2010

Living Well in a Down Economy For Dummies®

Published by
Wiley Publishing, Inc.
111 River St.
Hoboken, NJ 07030-5774
www.wiley.com

Copyright © 2008 by Wiley Publishing, Inc., Indianapolis, Indiana

For general information on our other products and services, please contact our Customer Care Department within the U.S. at 800-762-2974, outside the U.S. at 317-572-3993, or fax 317-572-4002.

For technical support, please visit www.wiley.com/techsupport.

Wiley also publishes its books in a variety of electronic formats. Some content that appears in print may not be available in electronic books.

Library of Congress Control Number: 2008933743

ISBN: 978-0-470-40117-0

Manufactured in the United States of America

10 9 8 7 6 5 4 3 2

WILEY

More For Dummies Titles to Keep You Living Well When Times Are Tough

401(k)s For Dummies, by Ted Benna and Brenda Watson Newmann (Wiley)

529 & Other College Savings Plans For Dummies, by Margaret A. Munro, EA (Wiley)

Auto Repair For Dummies, by Deanna Sclar (Wiley)

Canning & Preserving For Dummies, by Karen Ward (Wiley)

Cool Careers For Dummies, 3rd Edition, by Marty Nemko, PhD, and Richard N. Bolles (Wiley)

Credit Repair Kit For Dummies, by Stephen R. Bucci and Terry Savage (Wiley)

Everyday Math For Dummies, by Charles Seiter (Wiley)

Foreclosure Self-Defense For Dummies, by Ralph R. Roberts, Lois Maljak, Paul Doroh, and Joe Kraynak (Wiley)

Free $ for College For Dummies, by David Rosen and Caryn Mladen (Wiley)

Frugal Living For Dummies, by Deborah Taylor-Hough (Wiley)

Gifts from the Kitchen For Dummies, by Andrea Swenson (Wiley)

Haircutting For Dummies, by J. Elaine Spear (Wiley)

Home-Based Business For Dummies, 2nd Edition, by Paul Edwards, Sarah Edwards, and Peter Economy (Wiley)

Home Maintenance For Dummies, by James Carey and Morris Carey (Wiley)

Insurance For Dummies, by Jack Hungelmann (Wiley)

Job Interviews For Dummies, 3rd Edition, by Joyce Lain Kennedy

Personal Bankruptcy Laws For Dummies, by James P. Caher and John M. Caher (Wiley)

Personal Finance Workbook For Dummies, by Sheryl Garrett (Wiley)

Reconstructing Clothes For Dummies, by Miranda Caroligne Burns (Wiley)

Resumes For Dummies, 5th Edition, by Joyce Lain Kennedy (Wiley)

Slow Cookers For Dummies, by Tom Lacalamita and Glenna Vance (Wiley)

Stress Management For Dummies, by Allen Elkin (Wiley)

Telecommuting For Dummies, by Minda Zetlin (Wiley)

Publisher's Acknowledgments

We're proud of this book; please send us your comments through our Dummies online registration form located at www.dummies.com/register/.

Some of the people who helped bring this book to market include the following:

Acquisitions, Editorial, and Media Development

Senior Project Editor:
Christina Guthrie

Acquisitions Editor: Lindsay Lefevere

Senior Copy Editors: Sarah Faulkner, Danielle Voirol, Victoria M. Adang

Editorial Program Coordinator: Erin Calligan Mooney

Technical Editors: Joseph Nierman, Karen Bartholomew

Editorial Manager:
Christine Meloy Beck

Editorial Assistants: Joe Niesen, David Lutton, Jennette ElNaggar

Cover Photos: ©Corbis

Cartoons: Rich Tennant
(www.the5thwave.com)

Composition Services

Project Coordinator: Erin Smith

Layout and Graphics: Erin Zeltner

Proofreaders: Melissa Bronnenberg, Christopher M. Jones

Indexer: Broccoli Information Mgt.

Publishing and Editorial for Consumer Dummies

Diane Graves Steele, Vice President and Publisher, Consumer Dummies

Kristin A. Cocks, Product Development Director, Consumer Dummies

Michael Spring, Vice President and Publisher, Travel

Kelly Regan, Editorial Director, Travel

Publishing for Technology Dummies

Andy Cummings, Vice President and Publisher, Dummies Technology/ General User

Composition Services

Gerry Fahey, Vice President of Production Services

Debbie Stailey, Director of Composition Services

Contents at a Glance

Introduction

● ●

*A*sk an economist what a *recession* is, and you'll likely get the answer "a decline in gross domestic product lasting two or more consecutive quarters." (*Gross domestic product,* or *GDP,* is the total value of goods and services produced in a country.) At the time of this writing, America isn't officially in a recession (although many analysts say it's just a matter of getting the numbers that'll prove that the second-quarter decline has actually occurred), but the economy is definitely in a downturn. Home values are falling, employment is down, real income is down, and energy costs are skyrocketing.

So how long will this downturn last? No one knows. Some think it'll be over in a matter of months; others predict the recession could last a year or longer.

None of this is good news. Fortunately, you can do more than cross your fingers and hope for good luck. During a recession, you have the following main objectives:

➤ **Prepare yourself in case you lose your job.** As companies earn less, they look for ways to save money. Unfortunately, payroll reduction (read "layoffs and firings") is a key way to save. Fortunately, by preparing a resume and seeing this as an opportunity to explore alternative careers and ways to work, you can be proactive in protecting yourself in case you find yourself on the job market.

- ✔ **Take control of your finances.** Figure out what you have and what you spend and then make deliberate decisions about ways to rein in your spending. Your goal should be to live within your means if you're not already, to preserve your long-term financial goals, and to save enough to see you through a period of unemployment in case you lose your job.

- ✔ **Continue to live and enjoy your life while maintaining control of your finances.** The key isn't just to scale back but to do so in a way that you don't feel deprived. You can save a lot just by being a savvier consumer and by spending your money a little differently.

- ✔ **Have a plan to follow if the worst happens.** In uncertain times, you may find yourself, despite your best efforts, facing a financial catastrophe like a bankruptcy or foreclosure. Even in these circumstances, you still have options — maybe not many, and maybe not pleasant ones, but options that can help you weather even these storms.

Bottom line: In a stumbling economy, you have to tread carefully, but you can still move forward. This book helps you one step at a time.

About This Book

Living Well in a Down Economy For Dummies contains more than 125 tips and suggestions to help you through tough economic times. How can you scale back on celebrations without sacrificing the fun? How can you continue to save for retirement when you need all your income to make ends meet now? What do you do when college loans — or tuition — come due and money is tight? How can you save money on household expenses?

This book answers these and other questions for people looking to save money without sacrificing quality of life.

Each part of this book is divided into tips containing information relevant to that part's theme. The great thing about this book is that you decide where to start and what to read. It's a reference you can jump into and out of at will. Thumb through to glance at a variety of tips, or go to the Table of Contents to find the different categories of tips.

Conventions Used in This Book

This book uses a few conventions to help you navigate through:

- ✔ *Italics* are used for emphasis and to highlight new words or terms that are defined.
- ✔ **Boldfaced** text indicates keywords or phrases and the action part of numbered steps.
- ✔ Monofont is used for Web addresses.

Foolish Assumptions

In writing this book, I made some assumptions about you:

- ✔ You feel uneasy about the economy and want to get yourself and your family in a better financial position.
- ✔ You worry about losing your job, or you've already lost your job, and you need advice on finding work and cutting your expenses.

 ✔ You want to know how you can continue to plan for long-term financial goals like retirement and college savings when money's tight.

 ✔ You want to be a savvier, more thoughtful consumer so you can continue to enjoy life's pleasures without spending too much.

How This Book Is Organized

This book is organized into parts so you can find information quickly and easily. Each part represents a particular category of tips.

Part I: Facing Off Against a Recession

When facing a gloomy financial picture, the first hurdle is taking back control. You may not be able to whip the economy into shape by yourself, but you *can* regain control of your personal finances and attitude. This part provides tips that can help.

Part II: Bumping Up Your Bring-Home

A key challenge during a slowing economy is to ensure you have enough money to take care of your financial obligations. That means being prepared to find a new job, changing careers if you must, and coming up with alternative ways to earn a living if the traditional route (read "a 9-to-5 job working for others") isn't working out the way you'd like.

Part III: Putting Your Personal Finances on Firm Footing

Financial security doesn't just mean having a bunch of money in the bank; it means being smart about your financial decisions, especially during uncertain economic times. This part includes tips that help stabilize your financial position now and allow you to continue to prepare for the future.

Part IV: Living a Recession-Busting Life

The bulk of your income probably goes to your everyday home life. By cutting back on your household expenses — groceries, energy bills, auto and home maintenance costs, for example — you can save enough to put your personal finances on steadier ground. And here's a secret: Reducing household expenses doesn't require that you downscale to a pup tent and a pot of beans. The tips in this part tell you how.

Part V: Making the Most of Holidays and Other Special Events

Who says recessions have to be a drag? Nearly everyone, actually. But that doesn't mean you have to forego life's pleasures. This part offers tips on how to keep the good times rolling in a way that doesn't send your bank account into the red after every holiday or special event. In fact, you'll likely discover that being more thoughtful about what you spend results in more meaningful celebrations.

Part VI: Staying Afloat if the Boat Starts to Sink

Sometimes, despite your best efforts, things spiral out of control. If you find yourself facing out-of-control credit, bankruptcy, or foreclosure, your choices can determine how much you lose and how long it'll take you to recover. This part gives suggestions that can help you make the right decisions.

Part VII: The Part of Tens

Want to know ten ways to handle financial hurdles? How about ten ways to trim the money tree? Then this part is for you.

Icons Used in This Book

Many people, when facing stressful times, become very focused. In addition to myriad tips, this book uses the following icons to highlight information:

This icon appears beside especially important information: stuff that you absolutely need to know to make informed, wise decisions.

When times are tough and money is tight, mistakes are especially dangerous. This icon warns you about things that may have serious negative consequences.

Where to Go from Here

Whether you read this book from front to back or jump in and out as the need arises, you're certain to find a variety of ways to cut your expenses and stabilize your finances. Look at the Table of Contents to find general categories of tips, look in the index to find specific tips, or just flip through until something catches your eye.

Part I

Facing Off Against a Recession

The 5th Wave

By Rich Tennant

©RICHTENNANT

"It's really quite an entertaining piece of software. There's roller coaster action, suspense and drama, where skill and strategy are matched against winning and losing. And I thought managing our budget would be dull."

In this part . . .

Rising costs, falling income, uncertain employment, and no real idea how long the downturn will last: Harbingers like these can make anyone feel that economic stability is slipping beyond his grasp. Although it's true you can't control what's going on with the economy (even the Federal Reserve seems to be having a particularly difficult time of it lately!), you can take hold of your own finances and your attitude. And because everyone deserves a break during stressful times, this part also gives you some useful relaxation tips.

Determine Your Net Worth

● ●

A net worth statement is simply a listing of all you own and all you owe; the difference between the two is your *net worth*. Your net worth is like a financial report card. Knowing your net worth gives you a good idea of your financial situation.

To figure out your net worth, fill out the following worksheet. This information becomes a benchmark you can use to measure your current financial status relative to others and to where you want to be, from year to year.

Unhappy with your net worth?

If your net worth isn't what you want it to be, don't despair. Prioritize both your assets and your liabilities. Which assets are most important to you and your standard of living? Are there any you could do without? Which liabilities need to be paid off first? Consider interest rates and other terms for any loan you have, and then come up with a plan to pay down your debt. Part III can help.

Assets	Value	Liabilities	Balance
Cash Accounts Checking Savings Money Market Cash on Hand	$ _____ _____ _____ _____ _____	**Home Mortgage**	$ _____
Personal Use Assets Residence Personal Property Auto(s) Boat(s) Vacation Home Other	$ _____ _____ _____ _____ _____ _____	**Home Equity Loan/Line of Credit** **Auto Loans**	$ _____ _____
Investment Assets Brokerage Accounts Mutual Funds IRAs 401(k), 403(b) Other retirement plans	$ _____ _____ _____ _____ _____	**Investment Loans** **Margin Account** **Loans Against 401(k), 403(b)**	$ _____ _____ _____
Cash Value of Life Insurance Policies	$ _____	**Loans Against Life Insurance**	$ _____
Loans / Accounts Receivable	$ _____	**Loans / Accounts Payable**	$ _____
Deferred Compensation	$ _____	**Salary Advances**	$ _____
Total Assets	$	**Total Liabilities**	$
		Total Assets Minus Total Liabilities = Net Worth	$

Calculate Spendable Income

● ●

*T*o figure out your spendable income, first gather two to four copies of recent paycheck stubs and complete the worksheet that accompanies this tip. *Note:* Some deductions occur monthly rather than per pay period, so two to four consecutive paychecks should reveal all deductions. If you receive two paychecks per month and a certain deduction occurs only on the first paycheck, divide this amount by 2 when completing the worksheet.

1. Gross Income per pay period $ _____

    Minus:

    Taxes

            Federal $ _____

            State $ _____

            Local/City $ _____

            Social Security (FICA) $ _____

            Medicare $ _____

2. Total taxes withheld $ _____

    Automatic Payroll Deductions

            Medical Insurance $ _____

            Life Insurance $ _____

            Disability Insurance $ _____

            Dental Insurance $ _____

            Charitable Contributions $ _____

            Retirement Plan 401(k), 403(b), and so on $ _____

            Retirement Plan Loan Repayment $ _____

            Deferred Compensation Plan $ _____

            Employee Stock Purchase Plan $ _____

            Flexible Spending Acct FSA (Section 125) $ _____

            U.S. Savings Bonds $ _____

            Other Automatic Drafts for Investments $ _____

            Other Automatic Drafts for Expenses $ _____

3. Total payroll deductions (excluding taxes) $ _____

4. Net income per pay period (Line 1 – [Line 2 + Line 3]) $ _____

5. How many times are you paid per year?   _____

            a. Weekly = 52

            b. Every other week = 26

            c. Twice a month = 24

            d. Monthly = 12

6. Multiply Line 4 times Line 5 for annual net income $ _____

7. List traditional job-related expenses (annual)

Expense	Annual Cost
Commuting costs	$
Clothing and clothing maintenance	$
Child care	$
Unreimbursed business expenses	$

8. List nontraditional job-related expenses (annual)

You may incur these expenses due to the stress of your job, long hours, or working conditions. Examples include dining out frequently because you're working long hours, going out for lunch instead of preparing them at home, treating yourself to much-needed massage therapy or vacations to help decompress from the stresses of your job, and so on.

Expense	Annual Cost
_____	$
_____	$
_____	$
_____	$
_____	$
_____	$
_____	$
_____	$
_____	$
_____	$
_____	$

9. Total annual expenses on Lines 7 and 8 $

10. Subtract Line 9 from Line 6 for annual spendable income $

11. Divide Line 10 by number of hours worked per year (traditional full-time work equals 2,000 hours)

    Equals your net hourly spendable income $

Subtract Required Expenses

Your required expenses, or needs, must come first. To figure out what your required expenses are, fill out the next worksheet. (Sorry — no enhanced phone services, cellphones, cable TV, or high-speed Internet, unless required for employment, are included in needs.)

Cut back on unrequired expenses

You can reduce the amount of money you spend in all kinds of ways, and many of them don't require that you reduce your standard of living — only that you make more deliberate decisions about what's important to you and what you need. For example, consider the following:

✔ Can you change your phone package to eliminate the services you don't use and the fees associated with them?

✔ Can you downgrade your cable package to save money and still get the majority of the channels that matter most to you?

✔ Are you paying a monthly service fee to have a checking account? You don't have to; you can find lots of options on the Internet and in your community.

✔ Are you paying an annual fee for your credit card? Are you getting substantial value out of paying that fee? If not, cancel that card and use one that doesn't charge an annual fee.

Required Monthly Expenses (Needs)

Shelter:

Home Mortgage or rent $_____

Utilities:

Electric $_____

Gas $_____

Water, sewer, and trash pickup $_____

Basic phone service $_____

Protection: Include the things you can't afford to be without.

Life insurance $_____

Disability insurance $_____

Homeowners or renters insurance $_____

Health insurance $_____

Auto insurance $_____

Healthcare/medical and dental care $_____

Prescription drugs $_____

Child care $_____

Rainy-day fund (minimum of 10 percent of gross income) $_____

Food: This category doesn't include dining out.

Groceries (basic essentials only) $_____

Clothing and clothing maintenance: Presuming that you have some clothes now, ask yourself what else you really need. $_____

Basic Hygiene:

Personal: Toothbrush, deodorant, soap (for example) $_____

Household: Laundry detergent, toilet paper, and so on $_____

Transportation:

Automobile loan or lease payments $_____

Auto maintenance $_____

Gasoline $_____

Other: Tolls, parking, public transportation $_____

Legal Requirements:

Real estate and property taxes	$_____
Child support	$_____
Alimony	$_____
Required debt payments not listed elsewhere	
School loans	$_____
Personal loans	$_____
Credit cards	$_____
Other debt	$_____
Total required monthly expenses (Needs)	$_____
After-tax income (from previous worksheet, Line 1 – Line 2)	$_____

Note: If you included all expenses for the household, add
the after-tax income of both spouses/partners together.

(After-Tax Income minus Total Needs) **Surplus or Shortfall** $_____

Solve for Shortfalls

If you have a shortfall after you calculate your required
expenses (refer to the preceding worksheet), something's
gotta give. Consider the following suggestions when
you're faced with a shortfall:

> ✔ **Don't completely cut any required expenditures.**
> You may be tempted to drop insurance coverage
> and/or save the amount of money you need to be
> saving for a rainy day. You aren't doing yourself any
> favors by skipping these items, and the decision will
> come back to haunt you sooner or later.

✔ **Review each of the needs categories and consider ways to reduce necessary expenses.** You may be able to obtain less expensive insurance and save money on groceries, clothing, and transportation by shopping around.

✔ **Consider your employment.** Often, the only reasonable option you, your spouse, or your partner has is to increase income by working overtime (if that's an option), taking on a part-time job, or changing jobs.

Tracking your expenses is especially useful when your outgoing cash flow exceeds your income. For a clear picture of what you're spending money on (you'll be surprised how much you fritter away), keep a log of every cent you spend. Write down everything, whether you purchase a soda at work, buy gasoline on the way home, or go to the movies. Also track whether you paid by cash, check, or debit or credit card; who you paid; and whether the expenditure falls into the need or want category.

Create a Monthly Budget

Does the word *budget* send chills up your spine? It shouldn't. Budgets allow you to be organized and have some control over what you spend. They help you to decide how to spend your money, plan for your future, pay off existing debt, and save a few pennies each month by reducing wasteful and impulsive purchases.

Step 1: Categorize Your Expenses

When you begin setting up a monthly budget, start with big categories before breaking your budget down into smaller expense categories. A good list of basic budget categories to begin with includes the following:

- **Housing:** Mortgage/rent, repairs, property taxes, cleaning supplies, homeowner's/renter's insurance, utilities, furnishings, decor

- **Food:** Groceries, meals out, pizza delivery, snacks and beverages at work

- **Transportation:** Car payments, insurance, gas, oil changes, parking, repairs and maintenance, public transportation fees

✔ **Medical:** Insurance, out-of-pocket expenses such as deductibles and non-insurance covered medical services, pharmacy, eye care, dental

✔ **Clothing:** New purchases, dry cleaning, repair

✔ **Personal:** Cosmetics, haircuts, cleansers

✔ **Insurance:** Life insurance and any other insurance not covered under home, transportation, or medical expenses

✔ **Education:** Tuition, dues/fees, school pictures, yearbooks, school supplies, books

✔ **Credit accounts:** Major credit cards, department store cards, lines of credit through your bank or other lender, any other outstanding debt

✔ **Gifts:** Holidays, birthdays, graduations, weddings, showers

✔ **Recreation:** Vacations, movies, books, magazines, newspapers, cable TV, restaurants, sporting events, sports equipment

✔ **Savings:** Long-term and short-term goals, as well as retirement

✔ **Taxes:** Property and excise tax, for example

✔ **Donations:** Charities, religious groups, and so on

Be sure to set aside money each month for those yearly and quarterly payments that often sneak up on you when you least expect them. If you spend $1,200 on your yearly property taxes, divide that number by 12 and set aside $100 per month so you aren't caught off guard by your property taxes, insurance payments, or any other periodic bills.

Within each general budget category, some items are essential (the mortgage or rent payment, electric bill, and groceries); others are extra (new furniture, gifts, and pizza delivery). From your first list of general budget items, develop two separate budget lists, one for essentials and the other for extras. Then look through these lists to find flexible budget expenses where you can cut back by using the tips and advice throughout this book. Put a star next to these flexible items so you can identify them.

Step 2: Estimate What You Spend

Go through your checkbook and any other receipts or records you've kept over the past few months so you can track how much you actually spend on essentials. Then for one month, keep a detailed diary of all your extra purchases, even for cheap things like newspapers or coffee from the vending machine at work. Little expenses quickly add up to big money when they're made on a daily basis. These smaller, out-of-pocket purchases are frequently made with cash, so they usually don't show up in your check register; writing them down makes you aware of where the cash is dribbling out of your life.

For keeping track of your budget, take a look at office supply stores for an easy-to-use, inexpensive family budgeting book. If you want something small that you can carry with you at all times, the BudgetMap (budget map.com) is a specially designed ledger that fits in your personal checkbook and takes the fuss out of making and sticking to a budget.

Step 3: Calculate and Adjust

Are your spending habits keeping you in the red? To find out, add up the essentials list and the extras list separately. Subtract the essentials total from your monthly income. If you have money left over, subtract the extras total from that amount. If you still have money left over, great! Look into a savings or investing plan (talk to your bank or a certified financial planner for help setting up a plan).

If your extras list takes you into negative numbers, start looking for places to cut back (for example, cancel your newspaper delivery or eat out once a month instead of once a week). You can also trim from the extras list to put more money toward debt repayment if that's a high priority in your financial picture.

4

Breathe Away Tension

*A*s the economy heads south and you tighten your budget to keep spending under control, stress and tension creep into your life. You can't control the economy, but that's okay — truly living well is about far more than money. On the other hand, no matter how good things get, stress always leeches the fun out of the good life. Breathing properly is one of the simplest and best ways to drain your tension and relieve your stress. Simply by changing your breathing patterns, you can rapidly induce a state of greater relaxation. If you control the way you breathe, you have a powerful tool in reducing bodily tension and increasing your joie de vivre.

Change the Way You Breathe

Changing the way you breathe can change the way you feel. Here's one of the best and simplest ways of introducing yourself to stress-relieving breathing:

1. **Lie down or sit comfortably, and put one hand on your belly and your other hand on your chest.**

2. **Inhale through your nose, making sure the hand on your belly rises and the hand on your chest moves hardly at all.**

3. **As you inhale slowly, count silently to three.**

4. **As you exhale, slowly count to four, feeling the hand on your belly falling gently.**

   Pause slightly before your next breath.

5. **Repeat Steps 2 through 4 for several minutes and whenever you get the chance.**

Breathe through an Emergency

Breathing properly is no big deal when you're lying on your bed or vegging out in front of the TV. But what's your breathing like when you're caught in gridlock, when you're facing down a deadline, or when the stock market drops 20 percent? You're now in a crisis mode. You need another form of breathing. Here's what to do:

1. **Inhale slowly through your nostrils, taking in a very deep diaphragmatic breath.**

   Fill both your lungs and your cheeks.

2. **Hold that breath for about six seconds.**

3. **Exhale slowly through your slightly parted lips, releasing all the air in your lungs.**

   Pause at the end of this exhalation.

4. **Now take a few normal breaths.**

5. **Repeat Steps 1 through 4 two or three times and then return to what you were doing.**

This form of deep breathing should put you in a more relaxed state.

Tense Your Way to Relaxation

● ●

*T*he uncertainty of a faltering economy can tie anyone in knots, despite even the best of efforts to keep things in perspective, set priorities, and take control. Fortunately, one of the better relaxation techniques actually uses tense muscles to your benefit. It derives from a method called *progressive relaxation,* or deep muscle relaxation.

This method is based on the notion that you aren't aware of what your muscles feel like when they're tensed. By purposely tensing your muscles, you're able to recognize what tension feels like and identify which muscles are creating that tension. This technique is highly effective and has been proven to be a valuable tool for quickly reducing muscle tension and promoting relaxation.

Relax Your Body, Part by Part

When you have some time, follow these steps for progressive relaxation:

1. **Lie down or sit, as comfortably as you can, and close your eyes.**

   Find a quiet, dimly lit place that gives you some privacy, at least for a while.

2. Tense the muscles of a particular body part.

To practice, start by tensing your right hand and arm. Begin by making a fist. As you clench your fist, notice the tension and strain in your hand and forearm. Without releasing that tension, bend your right arm and flex your biceps, making a muscle the way you might to impress the kids in the schoolyard.

Don't strain yourself in any of these muscle tensing maneuvers. When you tense a muscle group, don't tense as hard as you can. Tense about ¾ of what you can do. If you feel pain or soreness, ease up on the tension, and if you still hurt, defer your practice until another time.

3. Hold the tension in the body part for about ten seconds.

4. Let go of the tension fairly quickly, letting the muscles go limp.

Notice the difference in the way your hand and arm feel. Notice the difference in feelings between the sensations of tension and those of relaxation. Let these feeling of relaxation deepen for about 30 seconds or so.

5. Repeat Steps 1 through 4, using the same muscle group.

6. Move to another muscle group.

Simply repeat Steps 1 through 4, substituting a different muscle group each time. Continue with your left hand and arm and then work your way through the major muscle groups listed in the following section.

After you finish relaxing each of these areas, let your body sink into an even deeper state of relaxation. Let go more and more. Mentally go over the sensations you're feeling in your arms, face, neck, shoulders, back, stomach, and legs. Feel your body becoming looser and more relaxed. Savor the feeling.

Use the Quickie Method

When pressed for time, you can use a quickie version of the progressive relaxation exercise explained in the preceding section. This technique compresses all the muscle tensing and relaxing sequences into one. Think of it as one gigantic scrunch.

In order to do this, you have to master the gradual version first. The success of this rapid form of relaxation depends on your ability to create and release muscle tension quickly, skills you master by slowly working through all the muscle groups individually. Here's what to do:

1. **Sit or lie comfortably in a room that's quiet and relatively free of distractions.**

2. **Tense all the muscle-groups listed here, simultaneously:**

   - Clench both fists, bend both arms and tense your biceps.

   - Lift both legs until you notice a moderate degree of tension and discomfort.

   - Scrunch up your face, closing your eyes, furrowing your brow, clenching your jaws, and pursing your lips.

- Bring your shoulders as close as you can to your ears.

- Tense your stomach muscles.

3. **Hold this total scrunch for about five seconds and then release, letting go of any and all tension.**

   Let your legs fall to the floor or bed, let your arms fall to your sides, and let the rest of your body return to a relaxed position.

Repeat this sequence at various points throughout your day.

Stretch Away Your Stress

Stretching is one way your body naturally discharges excess tension. You automatically feel the need for a stretch when you wake up in the morning and just before retiring at night. But a good stretch can drain away much of your body's tension at other times, too. You may be deskbound or sitting for long periods of time during the day, causing your muscles to tense and tighten. Consider adopting one or more basic stretches and taking a stretch-break at various points throughout the day.

Following are two tension-relieving stretches that help you drain off a lot of excess tension. They're simple and shouldn't evoke much comment or ridicule from friends or co-workers.

> ✔ **The Twist:** This stretch is great for your upper body. Sitting or standing, put both your hands behind the back of your head, locking your fingers together. Move your elbows towards each other until you feel some moderate tension. Now twist your body slightly, first to the right for a few seconds and then slowly to the left. When you finish, let your arms fall to your side.

✔ **The Leg-lift:** This stretch is good for your lower body. Sitting in your chair, raise both your legs until you feel a comfortable level of tightness in them. Maintaining that tension, flex and point your toes toward your head. Hold that tension for about ten seconds or so and then let your legs fall to the floor. If doing this with both legs together is a wee bit uncomfortable, try it one leg at a time.

Stretch slowly and don't overdo it. You're trying to relax your muscles, not punish them.

Find a local yoga class

If the deep breathing and stretching exercises in this Part appeal to you, consider giving yoga a try. In addition to the benefits from exercise and meditation, some yoga practices actually focus on things like contentment and abstaining from an attachment to possessions — two definitive steps toward living well, regardless of the economy! If yoga seems too trendy or New Age, remember that this practice has endured for thousands of years.

Lift a Finger for Self-Massage

• •

*W*ith all the stress and turmoil going on in the world and in your own budget, you could probably use a good massage to release some tension. Hold onto your cash and let your fingers do the work.

For Your Hands

Hold your left palm in front of you, fingers together. The fleshy spot between your thumb and index finger is a key acupressure point that should spread a sensation of relaxation when massaged. Using your right thumb, massage this spot in a circular motion for a slow count of 15. Switch hands and repeat.

For stress-related fatigue, pinch just below the first joint of your pinkie with the thumb and index finger of the opposite hand. (Pressure should be firm but not painful.) Increase the pressure slightly. Make small circular movements in a counterclockwise direction while maintaining pressure. Continue for 20 seconds. Release. Wait for ten seconds and repeat up to five times.

For Your Feet

Try this sole-soothing exercise. Take off your socks and shoes and sit comfortably with one leg crossed over the other. (The sole of your foot should be almost facing you.) With both hands, grasp the arches of your foot and apply pressure, especially with your thumbs. Knead every part of your foot (like you would bread dough, using your thumbs and fingers), working your way from your heel right up to your toes. Give each of your toes a squeeze. Now massage the other foot in a similar way.

If crossing your legs is more stressful than it used to be, go to the kitchen and get your rolling pin. Sit in a chair and position the rolling pin next to your foot. Gently roll your bare foot back and forth slowly for two minutes or so. Then try it with the other foot. Now wash the pin. If you don't own a rolling pin, work with a tennis ball. Place it under the arch of your bare foot, put some pressure on that foot, and move the ball backward and forward. Keep this rhythm going for about two minutes, and then switch to your other foot.

For Your Neck and Shoulders

Stress most often finds its way to your neck and shoulders. To dissipate that tension, take your left hand and firmly massage your right shoulder and the right side of your neck. Start with some gentle circular motions, rubbing the muscle with your index and middle fingers. Then finish with a firmer massage, squeezing the shoulder and neck muscles between your thumb and other fingers. Now switch to the other side.

For Your Face

Start by placing both of your hands on your face with the tips of your fingers resting on your forehead and the heels of your palms resting just under your cheeks. Gently pull down the skin on your forehead with the tips of your fingers while pushing up the area under your palms. Rhythmically repeat this movement, contracting and releasing your fingers and palms. You can also try pulling on your ears in different directions.

Practice Habits of Effective Stress Managers

*T*he following is a short list of the qualities most important for reducing stress and creating stress resilience:

- **Practice relaxation techniques.** You need to know how to let go of tension and be able to relax your body and quiet your mind.

- **Eat right and exercise often.** Be careful about what you put into your mouth. Engage in some form of physical activity regularly during the week.

- **Get enough sleep.** Try not to burn the candle at both ends. Get to sleep at an hour that ensures you can get enough rest.

- **Don't worry about the unimportant stuff.** Know the difference between what's truly important and what's not. Put things into perspective.

- **Don't get angry often.** Avoid losing your temper, but if you do become angry, try to remain in control of your anger so that it doesn't become destructive.

- **Get organized.** Feel a sense of control over your environment. A cluttered and disorganized life leads to a stressed life.

✔ **Manage your time effectively.** Be in control of your schedule.

✔ **Have and make use of a strong social support system.** Spend time with your family, friends, and acquaintances. Have people in your life who listen to you and care for you.

✔ **Live according to your values.** Make sure that you spend your energy and time on things that are meaningful to you and that your goals are significant and worthwhile.

✔ **Have a good sense of humor.** Laugh at life's hassles and annoyances. Don't take yourself too seriously.

If you realize that you currently employ only some (or none!) of the habits in this list, don't worry — you can change old habits and learn new ones. Managing your stress isn't a magical process; rather, it's one that means mastering new behaviors and finding new ways of looking at yourself and your world.

Part II

Bumping Up Your Bring-Home

The 5th Wave   By Rich Tennant

Tarzan - Lord of the Web

"...and then one day it hit Tarzan,
Lord of Jungle – where future in that?"

In this part . . .

*I*f you're thinking of ways to bring more money home because you've been laid off or downsized, are facing the possibility of being laid off or downsized, or just want to build a nest egg in case your financial situation goes south, you have quite a few options. In addition to finding other work — whether it's a new job to replace an old one or a part-time job to supplement what you earn now — you can increase your income by changing *the way* you work. Telecommuting or working from home is a viable option for many people. This part examines the opportunities available and gives tips on how to create and update a resume that'll get you a second look from prospective employers.

Update and Customize Your Resume

. . . .

*W*hen you see a job that you hope has your name on it, you won't have time to start from scratch and write a targeted resume that shows why you're the one to interview. The answer is to begin building a *core resume* — a basic resume that you customize — before the pressure hits. Use this resume as a base to spin off targeted editions when you need to move quickly. Constructing a targeted resume is easier when you follow this three-step game plan.

Step 1: Prepare Your Core Resume

Probe your memory to jot down every factor in your background that you could use to customize a resume, from experience and education to competencies and skills. This draft is your working model, a resume you'll never submit to an employer but a rich well you'll draw from time and time again. Use as many pages as you need.

When you begin drafting your core resume, consider the following four categories of essential information:

- **Education:** List your highest degree first — type of degree, major, school name, and date awarded. If you have a college degree, omit high school or prep school. If you have a vocational-technical school certificate or diploma that required less than a year to obtain, list your high school as well.

- **Experience:** Describe — with quantified achievements — your present and previous positions in reverse chronological order. Include specific job titles, company names and locations, and dates of employment. Show progression and promotions within an organization, especially if you've been with one employer for eons.

- **Skills:** Skills today are the heart and soul of job finding, and as such, they encompass a variety of experiences. In job-search terms, a *skill* is any identifiable ability or fact that employers value and will pay for. That means that "five years" is a skill, just as "word processing" is a skill; employers pay for experience.

- **Competencies:** A *competency-based approach* is a method that focuses on the skills, talents, and behaviors needed to perform a particular task to a certain standard. Although not all businesses use this hiring approach, some — usually larger, sophisticated employers — do.

Step 2: Research Job Requirements

If you're responding to a specific advertised job, jot down the requirements that the ad lists. Don't confuse the job duties and the stated requirements. Deal first with the requirements and then see how you can show experience or education that matches the most important job duties.

When you're not responding to a specific advertised job but are posting your resume in an online database, study many job ads to figure out the most commonly requested qualifications for a given occupation or career field.

Step 3: Customize Each Spinoff Resume

After compiling the requirements you must satisfy in a tailor-made resume, scour your core resume to see whether you can add secondary items mentioned in the ad that further improve your chances. Then start writing.

Never forget the resume-interview connection. To nab one of the better jobs and to move up the rewards chain, your targeted resume has to attract a decision-maker who will invite you to an interview to further explain how you can give that employer precisely what his or her organization says it wants and needs to succeed. If your employer wants A, you offer A. If your employer wants B, you offer B.

To accomplish this custom-fit hiring, make sure your targeted resume convinces the employer that your *value proposition* (a buzzword meaning *reason for hire*) is a perfect fit for the job, not a *maybe* fit for the job. Meet as many of the employer's requirements as you truthfully can. Admittedly, doing so isn't a walk in the park. In a world growing not only more global but also more complex, expect to do some head scratching and creative thinking from time to time.

Make Your Resume Stand Out

• •

*H*ow much are you worth to employers? When employment rates are stagnant and many companies are freezing or slowing hiring, you want to make sure your resume inspires employers to answer that question with "a lot." To do so, create a resume that's a compelling portrait of your strengths and skills.

Don't Tell It — Sell It

Basic descriptions of what you did on a job are boring. You want to instill excitement! List your background facts, but make sure you position them as end-user (employer) benefits. To sell your value and your benefits to an employer who has the power to hire you is to get specific. Communicate the importance of what you've done by using details — numbers, names, achievements, outcomes, volume of sales or savings, and size of contracts, for example.

Focus Your Resume

When your resume looks as though it'll collapse under the weight of a mishmash of jobs unconnected to your present target, eliminate your previous trivial pursuits.

Group the consequential jobs under a heading that says *Relevant Work Experience Summary*. If this approach solves one problem — the busy resume — but creates another, such as a gaping hole where you removed inconsequential jobs, create a second, abbreviated work history section that covers those holes, labeling it *Other Experience*.

Use Keywords

Recruiters and employers use keywords to search and retrieve e-resumes in databases for available positions. Employers search for keywords — chiefly nouns and short phrases, but also adjectives and action verbs — when trying to fill a position; they name the essential hard skills and knowledge needed to do the job.

When you use industry abbreviations (for example, "ROI" for *return on investment*), spell out the term at least once in your resume. Even though many systems are smarter than they used to be, a lot of older technology products out there won't get it unless you spell it out.

Massage Your Years of Experience

Sometimes a job posting calls for a specific number of years of experience — say, three years of experience. If you come up short — with only two years of experience, for example — but you know you can do the job, the basic technique is to work with what you have. Dissect your two years of experience and then add a statement in parentheses that says "skills acquired equivalent to three years of experience." The expansion technique doesn't work every time, but it's worth a shot.

Address Negative Perceptions

Even when it wasn't at your initiative, holding five or more jobs in ten years can brand you as a job hopper. Currently being out of work underscores that impression. Even employers who are guilty of round after round of employee dismissals instinctively flinch at candidates they perceive to be hopping around. Take pains to reverse that disapproval. When you draft your resume, post a list of negative perceptions on your desk; when you're finished writing, compare your resume with the list. Offer information that changes negative perceptions of you as a job hopper.

Get Acquainted with New Interview Trends

· ·

*A*re you having trouble staking out your future because you can't close the sale during interviews? Recharge with knowledge of the new trends and changing developments that impact your job interviews.

✔ **Expect new kinds of interviewers.** If the last time you interviewed you went one-to-one with a single interviewer, get ready for a different set of questioners, like a veteran team of six managers — individually or collectively; a hiring manager (especially in technical and retail fields) who's two decades younger than you; or someone of an ethnicity and heritage different from yours.

✔ **Be prepared to answer the direct or implied question, "What can you do for our company immediately?"** Because you can't count on being on the job more than a few years — or in contract assignments, a few months — the hiring spotlight lasers in on skills you can use from Day One.

✔ **Be prepared for a video interview.** Computer Webcams make it easy and cheap for an employer and job seeker to see and talk to each other no matter where each is hanging out — around the block or around the globe. Video interviews may also replace phone screening interviews.

✔ **Focus on fitting in.** Disappointed job seekers who ask employers why they didn't get hired are often told they aren't the best fit for the job. In the workplace, "fit" refers to how an individual fits into a company's culture. Instead of losing sleep over a fit-based turn-down, move on. Do better pre-interview research so you don't waste time on companies well-known for being a fortress of round holes when you're a square peg.

✔ **Cut the loyalty oath.** At some point you'll be asked, "Why do you want to work here?" The old "I'm looking for a home and I'll be loyal to you forever" statements don't play as well as they once did. Instead of pledging eternal fidelity, discuss your desire to do the work. Talk about how you're driven to funnel substantial amounts of productivity into the job quickly. Talk about wanting to use your superior technology skills. Talk about your interest in work that excites you, work that matters. Talk about work that — with its combination of work-life balance and stimulating tasks — is too tempting to pass by.

✔ **Revisit the dramatic pause.** A pause is effective body language and works great in face-to-face interviews. But in telephone or online video interviewing, dead air time can make you appear dull-witted rather than contemplative. Exercise judgment in using the reflective pause as a communications tool. (When you just don't know the answer immediately, that's another story; stall by asking for clarification.)

✔ **Polish your storytelling skills.** Interviewers ask candidates to tell them a story of a time when they reacted to such and such a situation. *How did you handle an angry customer? Can describe an example of a significant achievement in your last job?* The more success stories you can drag in from your past, the more likely those interviewers using this approach will highly rate your chances of achieving equivalent success in the future.

✔ **Learn new lines for small-business jobs.** As layoffs and downsizing increase, prime-timers are discovering that the small company sector is where the action is for them. Interviewers at big companies and small companies have different agendas. Emphasize different aspects of your work personality than those you emphasize when interviewing for a big company.

Stand Out in an Interview

• •

*T*hese ten super tips are sure to make the hiring gods favor you at job interviews. Read on to get hired:

✔ **Be prepared.** Preparation makes all the difference in whether you get the best offers as you face intense scrutiny, probing questions, and employers who are afraid of making hiring mistakes. You must show that you're tuned in to the company's needs, that you have the skills to get up to speed quickly, and that you're a hand-in-glove fit with the company. Fortunately, never before has so much information about companies and industries been so easily accessible, both in print and online.

✔ **Distinguish screening from selection interviews.** The purpose of the typical screening interview is to weed out all applicants except the best qualified. Screeners can reject, but they can't hire. During this interview, be pleasant and neutral. Volunteer no strong opinions. Raise no topics, except to reinforce your qualifications. If you make it past the screening interview, you're passed on to a hiring manager or panel who makes the selection. At this interview, move from neutral into high gear if the person doing the interview will be your boss or colleague. No more bland behavior — turn up the wattage on your personality power. This is the best time to find out whether you'll hit it off with the boss or colleagues or fit into the company culture.

✔ **Verify early what interviewers want.** Almost as soon as you're seated, ask the interviewer to describe the scope of the position and the qualifications of the ideal person for that position. The goal here is to confirm your research. If you're wrong, you must know immediately that you need to shift direction. Confirming your research or gaining this information on the spot is the key to the entire interview. This technique permits you to focus on the factors on which the hiring decision is made, without taking verbal detours that don't advance your candidacy.

✔ **Connect all your qualifications with a job's requirements.** If a quick glance at your notes reminds you that the interviewer missed a requirement or two listed in the job posting when describing the position's scope and the ideal person for it, help the interviewer by tactfully bringing up the missing criteria yourself.

✔ **Master a one-to-two-minute commercial about yourself.** Almost certainly you'll be asked to respond to some version of the "Tell me about yourself" question. For your answer, memorize a short description of your background (education, experience, and skills) that matches your strengths to the job. After briefly relating the facts of your background, add a sentence or two about your curiosity, commitment, and drive to build mountains atop your already good skills base. A few well-chosen words enliven a dry recitation of facts with a splash of your personality.

✔ **Allow the interviewer to direct the improv.** Some job search advisers seem to suggest that you take charge of the interview, directing the discussion in your favor. Not such a hot idea. Wrestling the interviewer for control can easily backfire when you appear to be usurping the interviewer's prerogative.

✔ **Try not to talk money until you know they want you.** When the salary question comes up at the beginning of an interview, say that money isn't your most important consideration (and it really shouldn't be at this point). Only when you know the scope of the position and its market value — and that the company wants to hire you — are the stars in alignment to bargain in your best interest.

Nail the Video Interview

*V*ideo interviewing (a form of videoconferencing) is a live, two-way electronic communication that permits two or more people in different geographic locations to engage in face-to-face visual and audio exchange. Miles separate them: sometimes few, sometimes many, and sometimes oceans. As companies look to trim expenses associated with interviewing and hiring, video interviewing is becoming more common.

The content of a video interview is much the same as that of an in-person interview, but the execution differs. For example, lag time occurs when data is compressed and sent from one location to another. Remember to allow for the delay and not step on the interviewer's lines, and don't be surprised if the interviewer inadvertently cuts you off in mid-sentence. In addition, you may feel performance pressure. When it's your turn to speak, you have very little time to look away, down, up, or sideways to process your thoughts. When the green light goes on, the pressure on you is somewhat like that on a contestant at a quiz show: talk or walk.

Here are some tips to help you gracefully navigate your way through a video interview:

✔ Send materials for show-and-tell in advance if the interviewer wants to ask questions about an updated resume or project.

✔ Run a technical check to make sure all video equipment is functioning properly.

✔ Pay attention to your appearance.

✔ Keep your movements calm.

✔ Introduce yourself simply and remember the sound delay.

✔ Look directly at the camera as often as possible when speaking.

✔ Let the interviewer end the interview.

✔ Sign off with a *virtual handshake.* You can say something as simple as "Thank you for interviewing me. I enjoyed it. Let's talk face to face very soon." When you're in a professional setting, push the mute button and leave the room. When you're at home, mute the mike and close the camera.

Make the Most of a Phone Interview

• •

*A*lmost everyone knows someone who's been contacted by a recruiter for a screening interview.
Sometimes the recruiter purposely tries to catch you off
guard, hoping surprise strips away the outer layers of
your preparation, exposing genuine, unrehearsed
thoughts and feelings. These recruiters also see unanticipated calls as useful for measuring your ability to think
on your feet. Because most people don't prepare for over-
the-phone screening interviews as rigorously as they prepare for face-to-face meetings, the casualty fallout is
heavy.

If you don't like surprises, schedule an appointment for
your phone interview. You don't want to answer questions on the fly when the call comes in because you won't
be prepared and you won't do your best. Instead, say
you're walking out the door to a meeting across town and
will call back as soon as you can.

Before your phone interview, make sure you have all your
essentials where you can access them easily during the
interview. Must-haves include your current resume, a list
of your professional accomplishments and brief stories
that illustrate your qualifications, background information

on the employer, questions about the company and position, and a calendar with all scheduled commitments and open dates.

When the time comes for your phone interview, follow these tips for optimal success:

- ✔ If you have a home office, use it. If not, take your phone into a quiet room stocked with all your interview essentials.

- ✔ Gather essential information from the caller.

- ✔ Don't rush or drone on.

- ✔ Be a champion listener.

- ✔ Get specific.

- ✔ Punt the salary question. When the phone screener asks how much money you want, evade the question for now. Wait until a face-to-face interview to talk money (see Tip #12, "Stand Out in an Interview," for details).

- ✔ Push for a meeting. As the call winds to a close, go for the prize: "As we talk, I'm thinking we can better discuss my qualifications for [position title] in person. I can be at your office Thursday morning. Is 9:30 good, or is there a better time for you?"

  When the interviewer agrees but can't set a specific time, simply suggest when you're available and ask when would be a good time to follow up. What you want is an in-person meeting. Assume you'll get it and give the interviewer a choice as to the time.

Look for Good Jobs Online

*T*he Internet makes uncovering hoards of job opportunities easier than ever; the trick is to find the right ones for you. As you launch your job-finding campaign, start with vertical job search engines as a destination for your targeted resumes; if you don't seem to be scoring winners, add general and niche job boards.

Use Vertical Job Search Engines

Vertical search engines — also called *verticals* or *VJSEs* or *aggregators* — are the job seeker's new best friends, and they're changing the online recruitment game in dramatic ways. You can think of VJSEs as "Google for jobs." That is, the verticals work as a search engine, except they search only for job listings.

With verticals, you go to one place and see virtually all the jobs that fit your personal criteria on the Internet. The best-known verticals include the following:

- ✔ SimplyHired.com
- ✔ Indeed.com
- ✔ Jobster.com

    ✔ GetTheJob.com

    ✔ Yahoo! HotJobs (`hotjobs.yahoo.com`)

Here are the general steps you're likely to follow when using a vertical search engine:

1. **Create a personal account.**

2. **Decide how often to receive the jobs: daily, weekly, and so on.**

3. **Set preferences indicating which jobs you're shown.**

4. **Become familiar with related options on the vertical site.**

5. **Narrow your search.**

6. **Track and save your searches.**

7. **Upgrade to an advanced search if you need it.**

Check the Job Boards

If you've been in the job market during the past 15 years or so, you probably know that a *job board* is a Web site where you can look for a job. Employers pay job boards to post their open positions. Job seekers typically view job listings for free.

You can apply through a job board for specific positions, or you can post your resume in the board's resume database. When you mouse aboard a job board, you can search for job listings by career field, occupation, job title, location, and job detail keywords. The emphasis is on *local* job markets because most people won't move for a job unless they have little choice.

You find job boards in two basic flavors:

- ✔ General job boards, such as CareerBuilder.com and Monster.com, cover all kinds of jobs.

- ✔ Specialty (or *niche*) job boards cover a specific group of jobs, according to factors like industry (EducationAmerica.net), geography (AtlantaRecruiter.com), or job-seeker qualifications (MBACareers.com).

Job boards are established hunting grounds for vertical job search engines. You can, of course, skip the verticals if you prefer and go straight to a job board. Many people do. Go to `www.topjobsites.com` to get the latest site rankings, which are published monthly.

Look into Federal Jobs

*I*f you've ever thought about looking into a federal job, time's wasting. Uncle Sam's 1.8 million civilian work-force (not counting postal service employees) averages 20,000 vacancies every day. Benefits are handsome: great health insurance, decent retirement plans, and flexible leave. Annual pay raises — often 3 to 4 percent — are automatic. You may not even have to relocate; many federal jobs exist in locales across America and even over-seas. The number-one way to spot a federal job that may interest you is to visit the official USA Web site (www.usajobs.gov). You can even search by salary.

As you pursue a federal job, keep in mind that federal resumes tend to be longer and require information not typically found on private-sector resumes. In addition, federal language is more bureaucratic than that of private-sector documents. Read the federal vacancy announce-ments (recruitment advertisements) carefully to get it right, and pay special attention to the qualifications and KSA (knowledge-skills-abilities) requirements.

Prepare for a Career Change

*A*s companies trim their workforces and more and more jobs are farmed out to contractors or sent offshore, even once stable and reliable positions are no longer so stable or reliable. If you've built your career in a field that's vanishing and now find yourself in the market for a job, the answer may be to change careers. Making a career change isn't the easiest thing to do, but it may be the smartest. To make the change, follow this advice:

- **Connect with others in your intended field.** When your change is voluntary, at least six months in advance of your leap, join a professional association of members in the career field or industry where you want to go. When your change is involuntary and you're suddenly left high and dry, scramble to assemble a skeleton personal network of people who can guide you into your intended field — and beef up that network as fast as you can. Make friends. Find out who's who and what's happening with professionals who can connect you with employment. Ask what you should read and which workshops you should attend. Ask whether you can visit a professional's workplace as an observer.

- **Educate yourself.** Seek out short-term certificate programs and workshops offered during industry conferences, as well as those available locally. If you study online, get the scoop on pluses and pitfalls about distance learning. One starting spot: www.geteducated.com.

✔ **Bone up on the industry.** Even if you're a nonacademic type who always sneaked light rubbish reads or sports sections into your study halls, you really can't afford to skip hard-core research on your proposed destination at this time in your life. Those greener pastures sometimes bleach out when something about the work isn't what you expect or can do well.

✔ **Talk the talk.** Learn the lingo of prospective new colleagues. You'll seem like one of them already.

✔ **Make the experience connection.** The bridge you use to join the old with the new must be rational and reasonable. Your qualifications have to come from somewhere — skills you already possess, volunteer work, part-time jobs, training, hobbies, and so forth. Strive to present a believable relationship between your qualifications and the career you're targeting.

✔ **Accentuate the positive.** Don't say you hope to change careers because there are no more jobs in your field. As in any job search, you're moving toward a preferred future, not running away from a bad spot or a toxic boss.

✔ **Tell true stories.** Expect to be asked the same kinds of questions that new graduates often face, such as some version of "Why shouldn't we hire someone more experienced in this line of work?" When you work out your answers, remember to use story-telling — that is, to back up your claims of superior qualities with true examples of achievement.

✔ **Take inventory of your core skills and knowledge.** Sort through to see which skills will cross over to a different industry or career field. Push them to the front of your memory where you can find and translate them as needed.

#18

Figure Out What You Really Want to Do

• •

*A*s in finding a mate, choosing a career should involve both your head and your heart. You may have a list of potential careers crowding your brain, but which of those makes sense? If you're like most career searchers, you're not sure. Answering these questions can help you figure it out:

- ✔ What is your worklife mission statement? In one sentence, describe what you most want to accomplish. If that suggests a career or a career must, write it down.

- ✔ Is there anything you absolutely must have in your next career? Think of these as the (almost) nonnegotiable items, things like a minimum salary, a prestigious job title, the opportunity for self-expression, a specific location, short training time, and so on.

- ✔ To be successful and satisfied at work, how do you want to spend the bulk of your workday? Do you want to spend it speaking one-on-one or to groups? How about reading, writing, or working with data, numbers, or computers? Do you want to work by yourself? Spend your time convincing people of something? Work with your hands?

✔ Describe your dream workday. Does that suggest a career must or even a career? Think what this day would look like from the moment you get up until the moment you go to sleep.

✔ What do you want your life to look like ten years from now? Does that suggest the sort of career you should pursue?

✔ Do you have specific expertise that you know you want to use in your career?

✔ What are your peak accomplishments?

✔ Write about the last two or three times you felt a surge of energy at work. Does that suggest a career?

✔ What do you find easy that many other people find hard? Many people aren't sure what their best skills are. The government-sponsored Skills Profiler may help (it's free at www.careerinfonet.org/ acinet/skills/default.aspx).

✔ What have people complimented you on that may have career implications? For example, have they said, "How can you stay so calm in that situation?" or "You wrote all that in an hour?"

✔ What are you passionate about?

✔ What is/was your favorite subject in school?

✔ If you wrote a book, what would it be about? What do you most enjoy talking about? The answers to these questions may suggest a possible career for you.

✔ Can you think of a type of organization that you'd love to work for?

✔ Is there a certain type of person you definitely want to work with?

✔ What career do your parents, partner, or close friends think you should pursue?

✔ If you didn't care what your family and friends thought, what career would you pursue?

✔ What career appeals to you that represents a dramatic change from what you're currently doing? Sometimes, what you need more than anything is a change.

Persuade Your Organization to Let You Telecommute

● ●

*T*elecommuting can mean big savings. Consider the expenses associated with a typical workday that would either vanish or be greatly reduced if you worked from home: commuting costs (including gas, tolls, and so on), dining expenses (breakfast from a drive-thru, coffee during your break, lunch, trips to the snack machine), childcare expenses, and other expenses like dry-cleaning for your work clothes. This is, admittedly, a most unscientific guesstimate. But if you're currently working outside your home, track just one week's worth of your own *in-office* expenses and add them up on Saturday. The total may surprise you.

The big hitch, of course, is getting permission to stay home. You may have the perfect job for telecommuting. You may have the perfect home-office setup. The benefits to your company may be impossible to deny. And you may still wind up with a nonnegotiable *no* for an answer. You can, however, stack the deck in your favor. Telecommuting, without a doubt, is a win-win arrangement, in which both employer and employee benefit. Use the following information to help your boss see why.

A corporation has human characteristics. Before it makes a major change, it wants to know, "What's in it for me?" Don't expect to get anywhere if your only answer is "a happier employee." Fortunately, that doesn't have to be your only answer. One recent survey, sponsored by AT&T and conducted by the International Telework Association & Council (ITAC), found that each telecommuting employee saved his or her respective employer an average of more than $10,000 a year by reducing absenteeism rates, saving the business money on recruitment and replacement, lowering facilities costs, and increasing productivity.

Although this general information is a big help when you set out to sell your boss on the benefits of telecommuting, you ultimately need to show how telecommuting can benefit your particular company, your particular department, and your particular job:

- ✔ **Examine how your telecommuting can help your organization reach its specific goals.** For example, if part of your company's mission is to provide excellence in serving its customers (a popular goal these days), working at home may enable you to deal with customer queries and complaints at unusual hours. This ability can be especially useful if your firm has overseas clients whose workday differs from yours.

- ✔ **Do a cost/benefit analysis to compare what your organization will spend with what it'll save by allowing you to telecommute.** The idea is to quantify some of those soft numbers and to demonstrate to your boss (and possibly upper management) exactly why telecommuting is good for business.

✔ **Demonstrate that telecommuting will work for your job.** When you can demonstrate that telecommuting will benefit your organization, your next task is to prove that it can be done by someone in your job — in other words, you. Begin by researching your own company's history with telecommuting. Your company may already have a telecommuting policy in place, in which case you simply have to demonstrate that you fit within its parameters. Then look outside your company to your main competitors and other companies in your field to see whether they allow telecommuting among their employees. Finally, find out whether others in your particular profession are telecommuting.

Find Telecommuting Work

*1*f your current job isn't compatible with telecommuting, or if your employer simply won't go for it, you may want to consider looking for a telecommuting job, particularly if you're dissatisfied with your current position.

Telecommuting Jobs

What kinds of jobs are available for telecommuters? The variety is huge and growing all the time. The following list provides a few of the jobs in which telecommuters are working on a remote basis today:

Advertising Copywriter

Animal Foster Home Coordinator

Business Consultant

Business-to-Business Materials Broker

Customer Service Representative

Fact Checker

Federal Government Worker

Graphic Artist

Meeting Planner

Mutual Fund Manager

Programmer

Public Relations Representative

Reporter

Researcher

Sales Representative

Stockbroker

Technical Support Person

Telephone Operator

Transcriptionist/Typist

Translator

Travel Agent

Job-Hunting for Telecommuters

Where do you search for your new telecommuting job? These days, many people conduct their job searches on the Web. It's is a great place to find a job, and it can be a particularly good source for telecommuting positions. But remember, it's far from the only source. Don't forget more traditional sources of jobs — and less traditional ones, too.

Search the Web

Finding the listings for telecommuting jobs on a general job site may take more work than it would at a specific telecommuting job site. On the other hand, you'll probably find a wider assortment of jobs at a general site. Here are a few of each to choose from:

✔ **Telecommuting Jobs:** www.tjobs.com

✔ **Monster.com:** www.monster.com

✔ **Workaholics4Hire:** www.Workaholics4Hire.com

✔ **Yahoo! HotJobs:** www.hotjobs.yahoo.com

✔ **The Wall Street Journal:** www.careers.wsj.com

Look for telecommuter-friendly companies

Where can you find telecommuter-friendly companies? June Langhoff's Web page (www.junelanghoff.com), the International Telework Association and Council's (ITAC) homepage (www.workingfromanywhere.org), and the Telework Coalition's home page (www.telecommute.org) are good places to start.

Also check out government jobs (see Tip # 16, "Look into Federal Jobs). Federal government mandates encourage telecommuting work arrangements, and many state and local governments are following the trend. Governments have a vested interest in combating air pollution, traffic congestion, and urban overcrowding. Telecommuting addresses all three problems.

Turn a traditional job into a telecommuting job

Do you have a former employer who's eager to hire you back? A local company that can really use your services? A job you know is a perfect fit and that you're sure you can do successfully as a telecommuter? Don't turn your back on a good job prospect just because your prospective boss assumes you'll be working onsite. You don't know that telecommuting is out of the question for this job until you actually ask.

Turn contract work into a telecommuting job

Many telecommuters start out doing contract or freelance work for the organizations that eventually hire them to fill staff positions. This transition is often easier to make than the one from onsite employee to telecommuter. This solution isn't right for everyone: Being a contract worker can be difficult, and not all jobs lend themselves to working this way. But it can be an excellent way to get your foot in the door on your way to a telecommuting position.

21

Consider Self-Employment

*Y*ou live in an era in which highly paid, secure employee jobs are increasingly reserved for super-stars. For everyone else, self-employment may be a more likely route. Do any of these self-employment categories excite you?

- Distributing the work of creative people: Examples include being an agent for performers or artists, being a film distributor, or owning an online art gallery.

- Replicating a successful business in a different geographic area: For example, opening a New York–style pizza place in the South or selling previously best-selling computer equipment in developing countries.

- Being self-employed in a high-profit-margin, niche field that has little competition: For example, selling used parts for 18-wheel trucks.

- Paying $10,000 to $100,000-plus to be shown how to run a particular business, step by step (buying an existing business or franchise)

- Turning people's complaints into a business that you can start

✔ Converting a hobby or personal interest into a business

✔ Finding a product or service that you want to sell

✔ Creating a template for a difficult-to-stage event and replicating it for different customers: An example is staging fundraising auctions for nonprofit organizations.

✔ Starting a grungy business, which means you have few competitors: Examples include commercial bathroom maintenance, hazardous waste disposal, and high-voltage electrical work. (Those aren't exactly cool careers, but sometimes making big money in a mundane career feels cooler than making chickenfeed in a cool career.)

But not everyone has what it takes. What about you? These questions can help you decide:

✔ Do you like being in charge?

✔ Are you flexible?

✔ Can you get things done?

✔ Are you good at solving real-world problems quickly?

✔ Are you persistent?

✔ Do you communicate well?

✔ Are you willing and able to market and sell?

If you didn't honestly answer yes to the preceding questions but are still eager to consider self-employment, you may want to work as an assistant to a successfully self-employed person. You'll either acquire the skills and mindset you need or realize that you're wiser to be employed by someone else.

#22

Get Acquainted with Home-Based Businesses

*I*f employment options look bleak outside your home, maybe the answer is inside your home: Consider a home-based business. Owning your own home-based business may be the most rewarding experience of your entire life. And not just in a financial sense (although many home-based businesspeople find the financial rewards to be significant) but also rewarding in the sense of doing the work you love and having control over your own life.

Starting and running your own home-based business offers these advantages:

- **You're the boss.** For many owners of home-based businesses, this reason is enough to justify making the move out of the 9-to-5.

- **You get all the benefits of your hard work.** When you make a profit, it's all yours. No one else is going to try to take it away from you (except, perhaps, the tax man).

- **You have the flexibility to work when and where you want.** Perhaps your most productive times don't coincide with the standard 9-to-5 work schedule that most regular businesses require their employees to adhere to.

✔ **You don't have to deal with as many distractions.**
You may find that — because interruptions from co-
workers are no longer an issue and the days of end-
less meetings are left far behind — you're much
more productive working in your workshop than in
a regular office.

✔ **You get to choose your clients and customers.**
When you own your own business, you can fire the
clients you don't want to work with. Sounds like fun,
doesn't it?

✔ **You can put as much or as little time into your
business as you like.** You can decide whether you
work for only a few hours a day or week or on a full-
time schedule.

These reasons to be on your own are just the tip of the
iceberg. When you add it all up, you're left with one fun-
damental reason for owning your own home-based business: freedom.

Admittedly, starting a home-based business isn't for
everyone. In fact, for some individuals, it can be a big mistake. If, however, you have an entrepreneurial spirit and
you thrive on being independent and in charge of your
life, a home-based business may be just the thing for you.

As you review potential business opportunities, be aware
of your own talents, mission, or passion, and keep them
foremost in your mind, because your success will be
directly proportional to the motivation that you bring to
your work. If you're a grand hand in the kitchen, for
example, you can become an sales associate for a business (like the Pampered Chef) that sells its wares through
home-based consultants; you can start a meal service
that sells prepared meals to busy families in your area; or
you can launch your own catering company.

Get New-Business Cash Flowing

• •

*E*very new business starts at the beginning. No matter how much experience you have in your current job or how many other businesses you may have started in the past, when you create a new home-based business, you're starting from scratch. The faster you get cash coming into your business, the better. If you're still employed when you start your home-based business, the sooner you're able to leave your 9-to-5 job behind. And if your 9-to-5 job left you, the sooner you'll be able to breathe a bit easier.

Start Part-Time

Few businesses — home-based or otherwise — bring in all the money necessary to get them off the ground and keep them going for a prolonged period of time within the first six months of operation. You need *a lot of cash* — from a current job, your spouse's or partner's job, savings, loans from friends or family or a bank — to keep both your business and your personal life going until the business generates enough revenue to take over.

Although you have to decide for yourself exactly what schedule to follow while transitioning into a home-based business, unless you're unemployed or retired, start your business on a part-time basis while you're still holding down your regular full-time job.

Finance Your Business with Startup Funds

It takes money to start a business. By lining up sources of startup funds, you're able to ease the financial entry into owning your own home-based business. There are probably more potential sources of startup funds than you can ever imagine. But where does this money come from? The following list gives several suggestions:

- ✔ Personal savings

- ✔ Credit (these options include a home equity line of credit, loans from friends and family, loans from banks or credit unions, credit cards, and microloan plans)

- ✔ If you use a credit card for your business, get one dedicated solely to business expenses. You'll have an easier time figuring your taxes for the year.

- ✔ Selling personal assets (such as a boat, extra vehicle, camper, and so on)

- ✔ Bartering (Craig's List, www.craigslist.org, is a great place to give bartering a try.)

- ✔ Disability grants

- ✔ Life insurance policies

- ✔ Local seed-money funds (such as one sponsored by the Amarillo Economic Development Center)
- ✔ Reduced tax withholdings

Turn Your Employer into Your First Client

If you're really good at what you do, what better way to get your business off the ground than to do work for your current employer on a contract basis? Not only will your employer have the benefit of your expertise while contracting with a known entity, but you can also develop your business while working with people you already know, using systems and procedures you're already familiar with.

Clearly separate yourself from your former employer as an independent contractor instead of continuing to work in the role of employee. If you don't make this distinction clear, the IRS may disallow any tax deductions you take for your home-based business.

Steps to Take before Leaving Your Job

*A*s soon as you're consistently earning enough income from a part-time business to cover your bare-minimum living and business expenses, you're ready to make a full-time commitment to your business. Before you turn in your resignation, however, take the five following steps:

- ✔ **Check when any company benefit plans you have will vest or increase in value.** If you have a 401(k) or other retirement plan to which your employer has been contributing, it may not be fully available to you until you've completed a particular number of years of service. Checking this information may help you determine the best time to resign. It'd truly be a shame, for example, if you quit two weeks before the value of your retirement benefits was set to jump from 80 to 100 percent.

- ✔ **Find out when you can expect to receive any bonus money or profit sharing.** You may, for example, be slated to receive an annual performance bonus or profit sharing a month after the end of the company fiscal year. This information can help with the financial planning for your business.

✔ **Get all annual health exams and routine proce-dures done, and fill all prescriptions, while you and your family are still covered by your med-ical/dental/vision insurance.** Check to see whether your group coverage can be converted to an individ-ual policy at favorable rates (some can be, although be very careful about changes in coverage, co-pays, and deductibles that may actually end up costing you much more money in the long run) or what other health coverage options are open to you.

Don't forget that if you work in the United States, you're likely covered by COBRA (the Consolidated Omnibus Budget Reconciliation Act of 1985), which requires your employer to allow you to continue your current group health coverage for a period of 18 months or more at the same rate (probably subsi-dized by the company) as all other employees of comparable coverage.

✔ **If you own a house, take out a home equity line of credit before leaving your current job.** Having a line of credit to draw upon is invaluable during the first two years of your new business, and your chances of getting approved for it are much greater while you're employed in a regular job. That's right — after you leave your job, you probably won't qualify for a line of credit or other loans for your business until your business has been successful for two or more years.

✔ **Pay off or pay down the balance on your credit cards while you still have a steady job.** This helps your credit rating (always a good thing) and pro-vides you with another source of potential funds to help you finance various startup costs (and depend-ing on the nature of your business, you may have plenty of those!).

Don't make your announcement or submit your resignation until you're really, actually, for sure ready to go. Some companies are (sometimes justifiably) paranoid about soon-to-be former employees' stealing ideas, proprietary data, or clients. This can make for a very hasty exit, with a personal escort, when you do resign.

Take Tax Deductions on Home-Based Businesses

*H*ome-based businesses pay self-employment tax (the government's way of collecting payments for Social Security and Medicare from the self-employed), state and federal income taxes, excise and property taxes, and miscellaneous local taxes or assessments. With all these taxes, you can easily be turning over 30 to 50 percent or more of your business's revenues to the government. Fortunately, you can take a number of deductions — some significant — for your home-based business.

Home-Office Deduction

For many, the home-office deduction is a major financial incentive to start businesses at home, and it can have a significant and positive effect on a home-based business's financial position (as well as the personal financial situation of the owner). For many home-based business owners, the ability to take the home-office deduction literally means the difference between success and failure.

The beauty of the home-office deduction is that it allows you to deduct the costs of operating and maintaining the part of your home that you use for business. And it doesn't matter what kind of home you live in. Whether you live in a single-family home, a condominium, a commercial building, or even a houseboat, if you meet the IRS's criteria for the home-office deduction, you're eligible to take it.

With a home-office deduction, you're allowed to deduct not only your normal business expenses (paper, pencils, phone calls, and so on), but also a portion of the indirect expenses related to your entire home! Examples of common indirect expenses are rent or mortgage, security system, housekeeping, and utilities.

To determine the total amount of indirect expenses you can deduct, calculate the percentage of your home devoted to your home office. If your home office takes up 20 percent of your homes space, you can deduct 20 percent of your home's indirect expenses.

Consult with an accountant, tax planner, or other tax professional before you take the home-office deduction. The rules are complicated, and the penalties for doing the wrong thing can be significant. For more information on deductions for your home-based business, check out *IRS Publication 587: Business Use of Your Home* (to locate this publication, enter "IRS Publication 587" in your search engine or go to www.irs.gov/formspubs).

Other Important Tax Deductions

Aside from the home-office tax deduction, home-based businesses are allowed to deduct a variety of other business expenses. As you may imagine, a home-based business owner can legally deduct lots of different things from his or her taxes. Examples of legal deductions include postage, auto expenses, Internet access, business meals and entertainment, retirement plans, interest payments on business credit cards, health insurance, and office supplies and furniture.

To be deductible, the Internal Revenue Code specifies that expenses must be *ordinary and necessary* for the operation of your business. So although the purchase of a vintage 1959 sunburst Gibson Les Paul electric guitar for $150,000 may be ordinary and necessary (and thus an allowable deduction) for a professional musician, it likely wouldn't fly for a home-based software designer — in fact, it'd surely sink like a lead balloon.

Ensure the Survival of Your Home-Based Business in Tough Times

*D*ue to your business's inherent smallness, you may not have enough clients to manage the financial roller coaster that can result when a customer goes bankrupt, puts you on a slow-pay plan, or switches vendors. Good planning can help you see far enough out on the horizon to anticipate the most serious financial shortfalls — and then take steps to avoid them — but anticipating all the bumps in the road and missing them when they arrive is impossible to do. Use the tips here to help you weather the storm and emerge stronger than ever:

✔ Save for a rainy day.

✔ Manage your cash flow.

✔ Keep in touch with your customers.

✔ Push your clients to pay their bills. You can figure which accounts are running behind by monitoring *receivables* — the money owed to your company by your clients and customers. QuickBooks and other business accounting programs have built-in receivables *aging reports* that make the task easy. And when you discover that one of your client's payments is overdue, act immediately — especially when the amount owed is substantial.

✔ Minimize expenses.

Be careful about exactly which expenses you cut. Do *not* cut expenses that'll bring more money into your business; instead, you may need to increase them.

✔ Offer a special promotion.

✔ Subcontract for others.

Choose between Itemized and Standard Deductions

● ●

*T*oo many people overpay on taxes because they take the standard deductions when itemizing would be better, or they itemize their deductions when the standard deductions would've been more advantageous. How do you choose which route to take? The answer is easy: Itemize your deductions if your total deductions are more than the standard deduction. For each dollar that exceeds the standard deduction, you'll reduce your taxable income by that amount. Otherwise, take the standard deduction.

Note: If you're 65 or older and/or blind, your standard deduction will be even higher than what you see here:

Filing Status	Standard Deduction
Individual taxpayer	$5,450
Married filing jointly	$10,900
Head of household	$8,000

Itemized deductions are limited or phased out if your adjusted gross income (AGI) exceeds a certain amount. For this reason, the value of your itemized deductions may not be as great as they appear if you fall into this category.

To determine whether the sum of your itemized deductions will exceed the standard deduction that you're entitled to take, add up all your anticipated itemized deductions and subtract this number from the standard deduction. If the net result is a positive number, itemize your deductions; if the net result is negative, take the standard deduction.

Figuring out AGI

Your AGI is your adjusted gross income, a number you need to know if you're planning on pursuing deductions. The quickest way for you to determine your AGI is to refer to your last tax return. You can find your AGI for the previous year on the first page of your 1040 return on line 37. If your income and deductible expenses aren't expected to change much this year as compared to last year, use last year's AGI for your planning purposes.

Boost Your Household Income

*W*hen you can't make ends meet with expense cuts alone, start looking at the other end of the cash flow equation: income. You, your partner, and any children you have may be able to generate enough additional income to soften the money woes that come with a dicey economy.

The following sections explain two ways to increase the household income — taking on another job yourself and putting other family members to work.

Make the Most of Moonlighting

Assuming your current agreement with your employer doesn't rule it out as an option, *moonlighting* (that is, holding a second regular job in addition to your main job) can be an excellent source for the extra cash you need. If you don't have a marketable skill, you can still earn some extra money by taking on a second job at a local restaurant or store. Do it regularly enough and you have a steady additional flow of income.

Don't plan on the extra money unless you always get the extra work or are very confident that you'll be able to hustle up side jobs. Develop a plan that *doesn't* take into account the sporadic moonlighting money, but use that money to help you reach your goals earlier than the plan calls for.

If you have young children, you may need to draw up a work schedule that consists of one partner working days and the other going to work when the first comes home in the evening. Depending on your family's goals, this can be a temporary arrangement until the family gets back on its feet.

Put Other Family Members to Work

During World War II, when manpower was short in the United States, women made up a significant segment of the workforce. When the United States was at war, everyone pulled together and contributed to keep the country running and our military overseas well equipped.

When your family is facing a financial crisis, everybody of working age can pull together and contribute his or her fair share to get the family back on its feet. If you have young children whom you're trying to shield from the problem, that's fine, but older teenagers are certainly capable of earning their own spending money and enough to cover their cellphone bills. Simply explain what's going on, ask them to assist you and be part of the solution, and share your plan with them. The experience can be valuable if they ever face a similar situation.

If an older child is extremely reluctant or refuses to help, tough love may be the order of the day. Older kids need to pay their fair share. Obviously, I'm not talking about asking your 15-year-old son to get a job bagging groceries and turn over his whole $87 paycheck each week, but you may ask your 17-year-old daughter to help offset the additional cost of auto insurance with a portion of her weekly check. Adult children should be working and contributing something toward the house payment, maintenance, and utilities; otherwise, perhaps *they* can find more affordable accommodations elsewhere.

Part III

Putting Your Personal Finances on Firm Footing

The 5th Wave   By Rich Tennant

@RICHTENNANT

"The first thing we should do is get you two into a good 401(k). Let me get out the 'Magic 8 Ball' and we'll run some options."

In this part . . .

You've worked hard to get where you are, and the fear of losing ground during dicey economic times can make you feel that not only is your current situation in jeopardy, but so are the things you've planned for your future: your retirement, your own or your kids' college education, and so on.

The good news is that you don't have to give up your future security or dreams; you just have to be smart about how you continue to pursue them. The bad news? There isn't any. Being proactive is the best way to be in control, and this part is full of information and advice about what you can do to protect your financial goals and find savings opportunities at the same time.

Avoid Unnecessary Fees

● ●

*H*aving a check returned for insufficient funds and being charged the penalties will certainly get your attention, but even smaller fees can take their toll on your finances. To avoid getting dinged for unnecessary fees, follow this advice:

✔ **Keep your checking account in the black to avoid overdraft charges.** When you write a check that bounces, you generally have to pay your bank's over-draft fee and a fee to the business you wrote the check to. If the overdraft results in a late payment, you have to pony up for the late payment fee, too. Things only get worse if the late payment is to a credit card company that ups the interest rate you pay.

✔ **Don't use your debit cards when doing so results in a fee.** If you use your debit card at a bank that's not your own, you may end up paying a service fee to access your own money. Some banks and credit unions add a charge when you use your debit card as a debit card (the transaction requires that you enter your PIN) rather than as a credit card or if you use it more than a certain number of times. These fees are easy to avoid: Go to your own bank.

✔ **Avoid cash advances with your credit card.** Many credit card companies charge a higher percentage of interest for cash advances than they do for other transactions. And because the card company gets to decide which balance it applies your payment to, it pays for the lower-interest transactions first, leaving the higher interest charges on the card longer.

Shop Around for Insurance

● ●

*W*hen you're buying any kind of insurance, do your initial research and comparison shopping online to become better informed about competitive rates for various policies. Then contact at least three sources and allow each company to provide you with quotes on a few different policies that may be best for your situation. As you question each company, be sure to consider the following:

✔ How much insurance you need

✔ How much you can afford to pay in premiums

✔ Special features or benefits, such as a waiver of premium, increasing death benefits, long-term care benefits, and so on

The three primary ways to obtain insurance quotes and products are through the following:

✔ A *captive agent* represents only one company, such as Allstate, State Farm, or American Family. It may seem that a captive agent isn't the best way to go; however, captive agents can be extremely competitive and provide exceptional customer service, especially for home and auto coverage. Yet these types of companies often aren't the most competitive in the areas of life, health, disability, and long-term care insurance.

✔ An *independent agent* represents multiple insurers. Independent agents can do a lot of comparison shopping for you and may be able to provide you with one-stop shopping for all your insurance needs. You still need to shop around, though. The difference in offerings can be huge even among independent agents.

✔ Buying directly from the insurance company is another option. Buying insurance directly from the company, without an agent, can usually result in savings of 10 to 15 percent. Don't count on any personalized attention, but you may save some money. However, think long and hard before you buy certain types of insurance, such as long-term care, disability, or medical insurance, without the guidance of an insurance professional, because these policies are often complex and require the guidance an insurance professional can provide.

Raise Your Deductible to Save on Insurance

* *

*G*iven all the insurance coverage you need — health, homeowner's, life, auto — insurance costs can take a large bite out of your bank account. Fortunately, you can reduce the amount you pay for insurance without jeopardizing protection. This tip applies to all insurance plans.

To some people, a lower *deductible* (the amount you have to pay before insurance starts paying the bills) means you "get something" from an insurance plan. Others point out that plans with higher deductibles are cheaper. In general, high-deductible plans are much less expensive than low-deductible plans. If you can raise and set aside the money you'd need to make your deductible, you can save on your insurance premiums.

Insurance is intended to cover risks you can't afford to bear on your own. The higher the deductible, the lower the premium. By raising your deductibles to $1,000 from $250, you may be able to reduce your premium by as much as 25 to 30 percent. Just make sure you don't raise your deductible so high that you can't pay that amount in case of an emergency.

Save Money on Life Insurance

• •

*B*uying your life insurance in pieces is a lot more expensive than covering all your needs in one policy. Plus, buying in pieces leaves you vulnerable to a gap in your coverage. Examples of piecemeal buying are having mortgage insurance through your lending institution, credit card insurance through your credit card company, credit life insurance with your car loan, supplemental group life insurance at work, flight insurance at the airport, and so on. When buying life insurance, figure out how much insurance you need to do the whole job and buy *one* policy.

In addition, don't buy policies you don't need or that don't offer adequate protection. Case in point: accidental death or travel accident insurance. With both accidental death and travel accident policies, you have no coverage for death from natural causes. Buying these policies is an especially bad move if you buy them in lieu of the full life insurance you really need. When buying life insurance, buy only coverage that pays for any death — natural or accidental.

Finally, buy life insurance when you need it, not before. Many single people have expensive cash value life insurance years before anyone in their life would suffer financially from their death. You wouldn't buy car insurance if you didn't own a car, so don't buy life insurance unless someone depends on you financially.

Some people fall into this trap, thinking they're saving money because life insurance is cheaper when you're young. This myth started because the *annual* cost of life insurance is cheaper *per year* when you're young because your chances of dying are lower. But the *total* cost that you pay over the life of the policy isn't cheaper. Suppose you buy life insurance for $100 a year at age 25 and your friend waits until age 35 and has to pay $110 a year for the same coverage. Now you're both 35 and you pay $10 less per year — but how about the $1,000 that you paid for the ten years that you didn't need it? Plus interest? Don't buy life insurance until you need it.

Qualify for Homeowner Policy Discounts

● ●

*1*f you want to qualify for a discount on your home-owner's policy, here's a list of things you can do to reduce risk, to reduce the chances of having a claim at all, and to reduce the severity of any claim you do have. You can also save on your insurance premiums by putting some of these tips into effect.

- ✔ Install a UL-approved smoke detector on each floor. Replace the batteries yearly. Also install a carbon monoxide detector.

- ✔ Install a UL-approved dry-chemical fire extinguisher in the kitchen for grease fires. Check it periodically to make sure it's fully charged.

- ✔ Have your fireplace, flues, and chimney cleaned regularly to prevent chimney fires (and all the horrible interior smoke damage that results).

- ✔ Install a central burglar-and-fire alarm (the premium savings are huge for this one — 10 to 20 percent).

- ✔ Install deadbolt locks on all access doors.

- ✔ Install a motion detector alarm.

✔ Install a sump pump system to prevent damage from groundwater, which is excluded by virtually every homeowner's policy. (Be sure to buy optional sump pump failure coverage.)

✔ If you have a swimming pool, have an approved fence. Take out the diving board (where most injuries occur). Add a locking pool cover to prevent unauthorized use.

✔ To avoid all the potential liability for injuries to the neighbor kids, buy your kids a membership to a health club offering a supervised trampoline instead of buying a trampoline yourself.

If you've already taken some of the steps that translate to a discount, make sure they're reflected on your policy. And ask your insurance agent whether any other discounts are available to which you may be entitled.

Take Advantage of Coverage You Already Have

A great way to save on your homeowner's policy is to take advantage of the coverage you already have and avoid unnecessary coverage:

- ✔ **Trailers:** If you own an expensive camping-trailer, you can insure it best and most economically by adding the trailer to your car insurance policy. Because car insurance covers only the trailer, add Special Perils contents coverage to your home-owner's policy to get better coverage for the belongings in your trailer in case of damage from a collision or overturn.

- ✔ **Instrument rentals:** Parents commonly rent instruments instead of buying them, especially for the child's first instrument. The rental agency requires you to insure the rental and offers you insurance on the $800 guitar you're renting — typically $4 to $8 a month added to your rental fee. That's $48 to $96 a year. You can schedule the $800 guitar under your homeowner's policy for $4 to $8 a year! That's the way to go — always. Be sure to include the rental agency as Loss Payee on the schedule so its interest is properly covered.

✔ **Valuables:** If you have any kind of property that's quite valuable and could be stolen, like jewelry or fine paintings, install a central burglar-and-fire alarm. Installation costs are often $200 or less. The monthly cost to monitor the alarm is about $20. You reduce the risk of losing an irreplaceable treasure, and you receive 10 to 20 percent off your homeowner's rates.

Look for Discounts and Premium Credits from Your Car Insurance

*T*he following are key factors that car insurers use to determine the price of your auto insurance and tips on what you can do to keep it as low as possible:

- ✔ **Age:** If you're very young or quite elderly, your risk of being in an auto accident is statistically much higher than for middle-aged folks. You can't do anything about your age. However, some insurers may penalize you less than others with regard to your cost of insurance.

- ✔ **Auto insurance claims history:** Safe drivers are rewarded with lower auto insurance premiums. Your history of making claims against your auto policy directly affects the cost of your insurance. The more you use insurance, the more your insurance costs.

- ✔ **Commuting distance to work:** The farther you drive, the higher your risk of being in an accident.

✔ **Credit history:** Insurance companies have determined that there's a direct correlation between your credit history and your risk as a driver.

✔ **Driving record:** If you receive a traffic ticket for speeding or another form of reckless driving, you pay for that carelessness in higher insurance premiums.

✔ **Marital status:** Married people historically are more stable drivers.

✔ **Place of residence:** Your zip code can have a drastic effect on your cost of insurance. Certain zip codes have a history of more auto theft, vandalism, and so on, and the insurance companies are still allowed to penalize you for living in these zip codes.

✔ **Type of car you drive:** A Dodge Dart station wagon versus a Hummer or a Corvette? The latter two require substantially higher auto insurance premiums because those cars cause or potentially receive much more damage in the same accident as the station wagon, and they cost a lot more to repair or replace than the older, less expensive vehicle. Also, drivers of sports cars statistically drive more carelessly than drivers of sedans.

✔ **Grades your child gets:** Most insurance companies give a 10- to 25-percent discount for a B average or better and another 30- to 40-percent discount if the student is attending college more than 100 miles from home and has no car at school. Ask for the Good Student and Distant Student discounts.

✔ **Other conditions:** Other things can reduce your insurance costs:

   • Having your home, auto, and liability insurance policies with the same company

- Having safety devices, such as airbags, antilock brakes, or an alarm system

- Not letting other people drive your vehicle (multiple drivers create multiple risks)

- Taking a driver safety course; many companies provide a discount to drivers who have taken a safe driving course

- Practicing defensive-driving techniques and wearing your safety belt

- Paying your auto insurance premium annually; most companies charge a service fee if you pay your premiums monthly, quarterly, and sometimes semiannually

Save on Medical Coverage Offered by Your Car Insurance

*C*ar insurance companies generally offer coverage for your medical bills. This medical coverage depends on your state's laws and generally comes in two flavors: Medical Payments (Med Pay) coverage and Personal Injury Protection (PIP) coverage.

The two forms of coverage are similar; they both pay your medical bills resulting from a car accident, regardless of fault, up to the limit you purchased. PIP has the added advantage (at a considerably greater cost) of also reimbursing you for some of your lost wages or *replacement services* (if you have to hire help around the home). Keep in mind three things when buying either coverage:

- State laws on Med Pay or PIP coverage vary dramatically. Check the law in your particular state.

- Buy only as much medical-related coverage as the law requires. You can save money on your insurance by buying no more than minimum coverage for either Med Pay or PIP. Medical and disability costs should be covered under other policies you have, so having additional car insurance coverage is unnecessary.

✔ Avoid buying additional insurance that covers your medical bills *only* when they're the result of car accidents. First, these expenses should be covered by other policies. Second, if you use this type of policy in lieu of a medical or disability policy, you're leaving yourself unprepared for medical expenses that are the result of other kinds of problems.

Continue Health Coverage When You Leave Your Job

● ●

*I*f you leave your job for any reason, you can lose your group health insurance. But almost all employers are required by law to allow terminated employees to continue group insurance coverage through COBRA (the Consolidated Omnibus Budget Reconciliation Act). Even though you must pay 100 percent of the cost of the insurance, this is your best option. If COBRA isn't an option for you, or if you're close to exhausting it (generally after 18 months), don't go without health insurance. Consider these options:

✔ **Individual health insurance:** If you're relatively healthy, consider an individual health insurance policy. To find a health insurance broker in your area, visit the National Association of Health Underwriters (www.nahu.org/consumer/find agent.cfm).

✔ **HIPAA:** The Health Insurance Portability and Accountability Act requires states to provide minimal coverage after you exhaust COBRA benefits, as long as you haven't had an extended break in coverage, which varies by state. Be aware that premiums under HIPAA may be two to three times the standard rate policy. Each state has its own HIPAA rules; to find out the rules in your state, contact your state insurance department.

✔ **Your state's high-risk health insurance pool:** If you're medically uninsurable due to significant health problems, apply for coverage through your state's high-risk pool (if it has one). To find out whether your state has such a pool and how it works, contact the National Association of State Comprehensive Health Insurance Plans (www.naschip.org).

✔ **Medicaid:** Medicaid is a federal program that provides healthcare services to the poor. Medicaid's eligibility requirements and benefits vary by state. Go to www.nahu.org/consumer/healthcare/topic.cfm?catID=18 for more info.

✔ **Local assistance programs:** If you're in a financial crisis, look into assistance programs that provide medical care at no or nominal cost. A small monthly fee pays for medical care at designated facilities for all family members.

✔ **State Children's Health Insurance Program:** SCHIP provides healthcare coverage to children whose families make too much money to qualify for Medicaid. Find out more at www.nahu.org/consumer/healthcare/topic.cfm?catID=19.

✔ **Federally funded community health centers:** These centers provide healthcare assistance to the needy. Go to ask.hrsa.gov/pc or call 800-275-4772) for more info.

Cap Your Out-of-Pocket Health Expenses

*M*ost health insurance plans contain some kind of co-payment on your part. Perhaps you have a co-pay per visit, such as $15 for each office visit or $40 if you go to the emergency room. Perhaps you have a deductible of $500 a year before your coverage kicks in (meaning that you pay the first $500 of your medical expenses each year). Or perhaps your policy pays 80 percent of all covered medical bills, with you responsible for the other 20 percent.

Paying the per-visit co-pays or the deductible usually isn't a hardship. But paying 20 percent of all your major medical bills in one year, without any limit on the possible amount of your contribution, easily can be.

When buying health insurance that contains a percentage co-payment, make sure the policy includes an annual maximum that's reasonable for your out-of-pocket expenses. For example, a 20-percent co-pay on the first $5,000 in expenses you have for the year is a $1,000 cap — with the insurer paying 100 percent of the bills the rest of the year.

If you have group coverage from your employer that has no cap on the 20-percent co-payment, you have a couple of options. If you work for a large employer, you often have more than one plan to choose from. See whether another plan has a cap. Otherwise, buy a personal Excess Major Medical policy with a large deductible. This policy typically pays 80 percent of your 20-percent co-payment responsibility.

Save on Individual Health Coverage

*T*he best way to save money on your health insurance premium is not to smoke or use tobacco. Unlike group policies, almost all individual policies differentiate smokers from nonsmokers because the claims costs for smokers are much higher. Blue Cross of Minnesota, for example, cuts 30 to 40 percent off its standard rates if you haven't used tobacco for three years.

You can also save on individual coverage by cutting out unneeded coverage, cutting back doctor choice, or raising deductibles.

When deciding between two deductibles on a health policy, choose the lower deductible if you're in doubt. You can raise your deductible later, anytime you want to. But to lower it, the whole family must qualify medically — not likely if you've just incurred some big medical bills.

Use Medical Savings Accounts

● ●

*I*n 1997, Congress created a pilot program called *Medical Savings Accounts (MSAs)* and made the accounts available to self-employed individuals and their families. An MSA operates like an individual retirement account (IRA) coordinated with a high-deductible major medical health insurance plan. Here are its features:

✔ Like an IRA, contributions are income tax deductible.

✔ Earnings on the account are tax sheltered.

✔ The maximum contribution per year is 65 percent of your major medical plan deductible for individuals and 75 percent for families. The insurance plan must meet MSA standards.

✔ From the account, you can pay your deductibles and most other medical expenses not covered by your health plan. Because the MSA money has never been taxed, you're paying those bills with pretax dollars — a huge advantage.

✔ If you've stayed reasonably healthy, you can leave unused funds on deposit and either use them in future years or save them as supplemental retirement dollars. If you don't use them for medical bills, withdrawals are taxed much like traditional IRAs when you do retire.

If you have interest in an MSA, check first with your agent or state insurance department. MSAs aren't approved in all states. You can set up an MSA wherever you can establish an IRA — banks, savings and loans, investment houses, insurance companies, and so on.

Tap into Temporary Health Insurance

*M*any states allow health insurance companies to offer the public *short-term* or *temporary* health coverage to meet short-term needs, such as covering a person who's between jobs or a college student who isn't covered by student health insurance during the summer. Coverage is usually available in increments of 30, 60, 90, 120, and sometimes 180 days. Coverage is usually quite good in many respects. Typically, temporary policies have a coverage limit of $1 million or more. They usually include freedom-of-choice and a maximum amount on out-of-pocket expenses.

The biggest advantage to a temporary policy is that you can qualify with almost no medical questions. Coverage can be immediate, if needed. But temporary coverage has at least five disadvantages:

- ✔ Preexisting conditions aren't covered. If you've ever been treated for a condition in the past, you won't be covered if the condition flares up again.
- ✔ The insurance usually isn't renewable.

  ✔ When the coverage period you've chosen ends, so
    does the coverage — often, even if you're lying seri-
    ously ill in the hospital.

  ✔ Claim payments are often delayed.

  ✔ Coverage outside the country is often excluded.

Because of major limitations, you generally want to avoid
buying temporary insurance unless you have no other
option. If you're between jobs, continue your group coverage from your prior employer under COBRA if you can.
And for summer coverage, keep college students continu-
ously insured under your family plan.

#42

Know the Tax Benefits of a 401(k) Plan

● ●

*W*hen you sign up for a 401(k) plan, you agree to let your employer deposit some of your paycheck into the plan as a *pre-tax contribution* instead of paying it to you. Your employer may even throw in some extra money known as a *matching contribution.* You don't pay federal income tax on any of this money until you withdraw it.

How much your 401(k) will be worth when you retire depends on a number of factors, such as which investments you choose, the return you get on those investments, whether your employer makes a contribution, and whether you withdraw money early.

A 401(k) lets you pay less income tax in the following two ways:

> ✔ **It lowers your taxable income.** The money you contribute to a 401(k) reduces your *gross income,* or *taxable income* (your pay before tax and any other deductions). When you have lower taxable income, you pay less federal income tax, and in most states, less in state and local income or wage taxes.

✔ **It enables you to defer taxes.** The gains in your 401(k) aren't taxed annually, as they would be in a regular taxable bank savings account, a personal mutual fund account, or a brokerage account (which you may use to buy and sell stocks and other investments). With a 401(k), you defer paying taxes on your investment earnings until you withdraw the money.

Continue to Invest, Even at a Reduced Amount

• •

*I*f money is tight, you may be tempted to stop contributing to your 401(k) (or any retirement) plan to bump up your bring-home pay. But you lose not only tax savings but also the benefits of the compounding.

The following example shows how you can cheat yourself by waiting just a few years to start saving or by stopping your contributions. Ken, Rasheed, and Lisa all earn $25,000 a year. They all decide to contribute 5 percent of their salary, or $1,250, to their 401(k) plans, but over different periods of time. Assuming that each has an average *annual return* (how much the money increases in value when it's invested) of 8 percent, look at the surprising results shown in the following chart.

Advantages of Starting to Save Early Through a 401(k) Plan

Year	A) KEN waits 8 years to start saving		B) RASHEED starts saving early, quits after 8 years		C) LISA starts saving early and keeps at it!		What you invest and what you earn
	Annual Investment	Year end value @ 8%	Annual Investment	Year end value @ 8%	Annual Investment	Year end value @ 8%	**A – started late**
1	$0	$0	$1,250	$1,295	$1,250	$1,295	**22 years @ $1,250**
2	0	0	1,250	2,694	1,250	2,694	Total saved $71,827
3	0	0	1,250	4,205	1,250	4,205	Amount invested 27,500
4	0	0	1,250	5,836	1,250	5,836	Investment return 44,327
5	0	0	1,250	7,598	1,250	7,598	
6	0	0	1,250	9,501	1,250	9,501	**B – started early**
7	0	0	1,250	11,557	1,250	11,557	**8 years @ $1,250**
8	0	0	1,250	13,777	1,250	13,777	Total saved $71,827
9	1,250	1,295	0	14,879	1,250	16,174	Amount invested 27,500
10	1,250	2,694	0	16,069	1,250	18,763	Investment return 44,327
15	1,250	11,557	0	23,611	1,250	35,167	**C – started early & continued**
20	1,250	24,579	0	34,692	1,250	59,271	**30 years @ $1,250**
25	1,250	43,713	0	50,973	1,250	94,687	Total saved $71,827
							Amount invested 27,500
30	1,250	71,827	0	74,897	1,250	146,724	Investment return 44,327

The figures indicated reflect employee contributions only. In this example, investment return is calculated at 8%. Your own 401(k) investment return may be higher or lower, depending on the performance of the funds offered and how you invested the money in your account.

You can see that it pays to start saving early and to keep saving. In this example, each person is saving a little more than $100 per month. If that seems like too much for you now, consider contributing a smaller amount. Sometimes that's the best way to get started or to keep going.

If you absolutely must scale back your 401(k) contributions due to financial hardship, factor in whether your employer matches your contribution. If it does, lower your contribution only as far as your employer matches; otherwise, you're doing yourself a double disservice.

Borrow from Your 401(k)

*Y*ou can borrow from your 401(k) only if your plan document allows you to borrow for the specific reason you have in mind. Some plans permit borrowing for any reason, but most permit loans only for the reasons included on the hardship withdrawal list. Get details about account loans from your summary plan description, your benefits office, or 401(k) plan provider.

Figure Out How Much You Can Borrow

The government sets the limits on how much you can borrow. Generally, you're allowed to borrow no more than 50 percent of your account value up to $50,000 maximum. The other half stays in the account as collateral. However, government rules theoretically permit borrowing 100 percent of an account up to $10,000. So if your account value is $15,000, you may be able to borrow $10,000, even though 50 percent of $15,000 is only $7,500. Most plans don't allow this; they limit all loans to 50 percent of the account value for the sake of simplicity. Some plans also impose a minimum loan amount because administering a loan for only a few bucks isn't worth the hassle.

Determine How Much Interest You'll Pay

The interest you pay on your 401(k) loan is determined by your employer and must be a level that meets IRS requirements. It's usually the *prime rate* (the interest rate banks charge the most creditworthy companies) plus 1 or 2 percentage points. In most plans, the interest you pay goes back into your account, so you're in the interesting position of being both the borrower and the lender.

Repayment Rules

You normally have to repay the loan within five years, but you can repay it faster if your plan permits. Your employer may permit a longer repayment period if you use the money for a home purchase.

Employers usually require you to repay a loan through deductions from your paycheck. The loan repayments are taken out of your paycheck after taxes, not pre-tax like your original contributions. Then, when you eventually withdraw this money in retirement, you pay tax on it again. This point bears repeating: *You pay tax twice on money used to repay a 401(k) loan.*

Most employers require you to pay back the loan with payroll deductions, so if you're laid off or you quit your job, continuing to repay the loan becomes impossible. You can either repay the entire outstanding loan balance right away or take the amount as a taxable *distribution* (payment from the account).

If you don't have the money to repay the loan, you have to declare the entire unpaid loan balance as income on your tax return. Adding insult to injury, if you're younger than 55 when you leave your job, you'll probably have to pay an early withdrawal penalty of 10 percent or more.

If you take a loan, continue to make pre-tax contributions to your 401(k) while repaying the loan. If you don't, your eventual account balance will be lower than if you hadn't taken the loan. Say you're contributing $1,800 a year pre-tax to your 401(k) and you receive an employer matching contribution of $900. If you stop contributing for five years (the loan repayment period), you lose out on $9,000 of your own contributions ($1,800 × 5) and $4,500 in employer matching contributions ($900 × 5). If you invest those amounts in the 401(k) plan over 30 years, with an average return of 9 percent, they grow to $139,340.

Let Your 401(k) Roll Over to Avoid Taxes

*W*hen you leave your job, one of the many forms that you'll likely have to fill out is a 401(k) *distribution election form*. (*Distribution* is employee-benefit-speak for the payment of your vested 401(k) money to you.)

The most sensible thing to do with your 401(k) from a tax-management point of view is a *direct rollover* (also known as a *trustee-to-trustee transfer*) of the money. With this type of rollover, the money goes directly from your 401(k) plan into another tax-deferred account — an individual retirement account (IRA) or your new employer's plan. By doing a direct rollover, you don't have to pay any tax on the money when it comes out of your old employer's 401(k). The money also continues to grow tax-deferred in the new account.

Roll Over into an IRA

You can roll money from your 401(k) into a traditional IRA. When rolling over into an IRA, you can do a *partial rollover,* rolling over only part of your 401(k) while leaving the rest in your 401(k) account or cashing it out. For example, you may not want to roll over employer stock if you receive shares as part of your distribution. Or you may withdraw some of your 401(k) money right away to pay for an expense but roll the remainder into an IRA to keep it working for your retirement.

If you already have a traditional IRA, you can roll your 401(k) money into that account. However, it's probably a better idea to open a separate IRA just for your rollover money. This makes keeping track of the funds easier. This type of account is often referred to as a *conduit IRA* because it can act as a conduit between your old 401(k) and a new employer's plan or a *rollover IRA*.

You can't roll your 401(k) directly into a Roth IRA. (This is because a Roth IRA is treated differently for tax purposes.) What you may be able to do, however, if you really want a Roth, is convert your traditional IRA into a Roth after doing the rollover. You can do a partial conversion of a traditional IRA into a Roth — leaving some of the traditional IRA intact. Because you pay income tax on the converted amount, reducing the amount you convert lowers the tax you pay for the conversion.

Roll Over into Another Employer's Plan

You may be able to roll the money over into your new employer's plan. You may decide to do this for a number of reasons, including

✔ Your new employer has a terrific plan with great funds and low expenses.

✔ You want to consolidate all your retirement savings in one place for ease of management.

✔ You think you may want to take a loan someday (you can't take a loan from an IRA).

Your new plan may require you to wait until you're eligible to participate before accepting a rollover from your old 401(k). If, for example, your new employer has a waiting period of one year before you can contribute to the 401(k), you have to wait one year to roll the money into the 401(k). In that case, you can either leave your money in your former employer's plan or move it to a conduit IRA, ready to be transferred into the new 401(k) when the time comes.

Investigate Tax-Deferred Ways to Save for College

• •

*S*aving money is a good thing, even when financial times are tough. Uncle Sam is prepared to back up that philosophy with a variety of savings programs that contain built-in tax incentives.

Section 529 Plans

Qualified tuition programs covered under Section 529 of the Internal Revenue Code allow you to save money or purchase tuition credits for future college expenses for a specific beneficiary. Your money goes into an account that's administered either by the state (yours or any other — some states allow residents of other states to participate in their plans) or by a specific college or university. You may see them called either *Section 529 plans* or *qualified tuition programs* — they're one and the same. These savings plans can be a fantastic way to save for future educational expenses. To make a plan work, though, you have to understand its requirements and follow them.

When you make a contribution to a Section 529 plan, you're not allowed any federal income tax deduction for the amount of your contribution (unlike many sorts of retirement plans, which defer income tax not only on the accrued earnings in the account but also on your contributions). Depending on which state you live in (and if you use its plan), you may get a current state income tax deduction for part or all of your contribution each year.

After your money is safely tied up in a Section 529 plan, interest that you earn on it isn't taxed until distributions are made to your designated beneficiary. And if you use these distributions to pay the qualified education expenses of a student at an eligible educational institution, accrued earnings generally aren't taxed at all. In other words, a Section 529 plan allows you to save for college, and it exempts or defers income tax on the accrued earnings until the designated beneficiary begins taking distributions from the plan.

To get these tax benefits, the expenses must be used for qualified expenses (tuition, room and board, books, and so on) at qualified institutions, such as postsecondary schools eligible to participate in U.S. Department of Education financial aid programs, many vocational and technical schools, community colleges, and so on.

Coverdell Accounts

Coverdell education savings accounts (ESAs) also enable you to save now for future educational expenses — whether primary, secondary, or postsecondary — of a designated beneficiary. You can invest money in Coverdell accounts in a variety of ways: stocks, bonds, money market accounts, certificates of deposit, and so on, although you may not invest in life insurance policies. Under the Coverdell rules (and unlike Section 529 rules), if you designate yourself the one responsible for all decisions on this particular account, you keep control of the money and make all the investment decisions for your child's account. Over the years, the investments will hopefully earn significant income through interest, dividends, and capital gains, until the time the account is closed.

You pay no income tax on the income when it's earned, and as distributions are made from these accounts to your designated beneficiary for qualified educational expenses, the income portion of the distribution isn't taxed, either to you or to your student.

Squeeze Out Every Drop of Available College Money

*A*fter you begin to suspect that your savings and amounts available from current earnings will fall short of your child's anticipated educational costs, some planning may well increase the amount of outright grants and very low-cost loans your student may qualify for.

Time the Receipt of Taxable and Tax-Exempt Income

Do your best to schedule large infusions of income and cash two years or more before your child is due to start college; the financial aid folks won't care about what's on your income tax return in any years other than your base years (the calendar years used to determine how much financial aid you receive). So if you need to sell an investment, do it sooner rather than later. If you're going to receive a year-end bonus, try to defer it to a non-base year if possible. You want to avoid large amounts of extra income in your base years.

Pay Down Debt

The folks who process your FAFSA (Free Application for Federal Student Aid; see www.fafsa.ed.gov) are concerned with how much you have in income and assets, not how much you owe, which means you don't even get any credit for your debts. So to minimize the value of assets you show on your aid application, get rid of your debt. Sell some assets, if necessary, to pay off your car loan, make extra mortgage payments, and bring your credit card balances to zero. Complete all these transactions before you fill in your aid applications; the FAFSA folks are concerned only with the value of your assets on the day that you complete the application — not the day before and not the day after. Your good intentions will be worth less than nothing if you raise the cash but fail to pay off your debt before filing your application.

Get Assets Out of Your Child's Name

The financial aid people include at most 5.6 percent of parents' includable assets in their calculation of *expected family contribution* (EFC), the amount that the U.S. Department of Education figures you should be able to cough up for one child's educational costs in any given year. They expect your child to kick in a whopping 35 percent of her assets as part of the same EFC for one year.

If you want to minimize the amount of your EFC, keep assets in your name alone, joint with your spouse, or in the name of another relative outside the household. If your child has accumulated assets since birth — for example, in a Coverdell ESA (see Tip #46, "Investigate Tax-Deferred Ways to Save for College," for more on Coverdell accounts) — spend down these assets first.

Anticipate Your Expenses

Most people have large expenses they tend to postpone, such as replacing a car or a roof, when facing the first college tuition bill. But while a certain amount of self-deprivation is normal for parents, indulging yourself a little may actually help your student's overall financial aid picture. Replace that old rust bucket that's been held together with duct tape for the last three years (but remember, pay cash — don't finance it unless you absolutely must), and repair the roof. Paying for these items depletes your cash and asset balances, which you must, of course, report accurately on the FAFSA. Because the value of the new car and the house repairs isn't included on your aid application, you can successfully convert reportable assets into nonreportable assets and also take care of some necessary expenses in the process.

Spread Your Available Assets across Multiple Students

You may be surprised to find out that although each of your children has to file his or her own FAFSA application, your EFC isn't the same for each student. The portion of the EFC that's calculated based on your income is divided by the number of students you currently have in college. The student's portion (based on his income and assets) is then added on each application, arriving at the

EFC for each student. The more members of your family who are attending a postsecondary school at any given time, the greater the potential financial aid award for each student. Although the total that you'll be expected to pay will likely be greater for multiple students than it would be if you just had one in school, the per-student cost should be less (unless your income and/or asset value is very large).

Look into Federal Assistance Programs

• •

*T*he U.S. Department of Education will give out approximately 83 billion dollars this year to help students and their families afford the steep costs of university, college, and trade school. This whopping amount represents roughly 60 percent of *all* student aid disbursed, so it's an obvious place to start looking for free money. To access these monies, you need to fill out the FAFSA (Free Application for Federal Student Aid).

Federal Pell Grants

Pell grants are designed for undergraduate students who haven't yet earned a bachelor's or professional degree — and this includes high school students heading into their first year of college. These grants, which are given to students based on need, are especially great because they don't have to be repaid. *Note: Need* is defined as the difference between what a student (and her parents or guardians) *can* pay and the actual cost of her education.

No matter how desperate your financial position, the most you can expect from the Federal Pell Grant program is $4,050 per year.

Federal Supplemental Educational Opportunity Grant

The FSEOG is a program designed for undergraduate students with "exceptional financial need." In plain English, these students have to have a very low expected family contribution (EFC), due to obvious poverty or immense financial drain on their parents (such as supporting lots of other kids in college or caring for elderly parents). The first students to get any money from the FSEOG program are Pell Grant recipients with the lowest EFCs. Like the Pell Grant, FSEOG monies don't have to be paid back.

If you qualify, you can get between $100 and $4,000 a year, depending on when you apply, your financial need, and the funding offered at the school you're attending. Only undergraduate students who haven't earned a bachelor's or a professional degree are eligible for FSEOG awards.

Hope Scholarship and Lifetime Learning Credits

Two of the best tax incentives aimed at middle class parents of college students are the *Hope Scholarship Credit* and the *Lifetime Learning Credit.* Both of these programs offer tax credits to partially compensate parents (or other tuition payers) for paying their dependent students' college tuition. Independent students can also qualify for these credits. With these credits, you can deduct a certain amount of your education costs from your annual income to get a break on your taxes. For more information on the Hope Scholarship Credit and the Lifetime Learning Credit, go to www.irs.gov/faqs/faq7-4.html.

Make Use of Federal Loans

*F*our major types of federal loans are available to students or their parents: Stafford Loans, PLUS Loans, Perkins Loans, and Consolidation Loans. Each type of loan is aimed at a different set of people, each has its own interest rate and repayment terms, and each has its own advantages and disadvantages.

Some loans are *subsidized,* which means you don't pay interest on them until you graduate or otherwise leave school. In other cases, the loans are *unsubsidized,* meaning you're charged interest from the day the loan is sent to you to the day you pay it back. Unsubsidized loans are less advantageous than their subsidized counterparts because subsidized loans give you a free ride, without the need to service the debt (in other words, pay interest) while you're in school.

All federal student aid (as well as state and college aid) begins with the completion of the FAFSA.

Stafford Loans

Stafford Loans come from two different sources: either the federal government or third-party lending institutions. Each school chooses to use its money from the Stafford program in one of these two ways:

- ✔ The school uses the *Direct Loan Program,* in which the U.S. government directly loans you the money you need for school. Under this program, the federal government is your lender and you repay the loan to Uncle Sam.

- ✔ The school disburses Stafford Loans in which the U.S. government indirectly loans you the money through its *Federal Family Education Loan* (FFEL) Program. Under this program, third-party lenders such as banks, credit unions, and other institutions are your lenders and you repay them.

Stafford Loans are either subsidized or unsubsidized. With a subsidized Stafford Loan, you won't be charged any interest until after you graduate, drop out, or leave school for other reasons. These loans are awarded to students with low expected family contribution (EFC) amounts, based on the information they supply in their FAFSAs. Unsubsidized Stafford Loans charge interest from the time they're disbursed until you completely pay them off. By law, the interest rate on your Stafford Loan can't exceed 8.25 percent, and the actual rate is fixed once a year in late June.

PLUS Loans

PLUS is an acronym for *Parent Loans for Undergraduate Students.* You can probably guess that these loans are aimed at parents of kids who are undergraduate students at colleges. To qualify for PLUS Loans, parents must have children who are enrolled at least half-time at an approved educational institution. By law, interest rates for PLUS Loans are set once a year but can never exceed 9 percent.

Similar to Stafford Loans, PLUS Loans have a maximum allowable amount that can be borrowed: that maximum is the difference between the cost of the student's attendance and any other financial aid the student receives (a number set by the school's financial aid office). If the cost for the student to attend college is $7,000 and he receives $4,500 in financial aid from other sources, his parents can borrow up to $2,500.

Unlike Stafford Loans, PLUS Loans feature neither a grace period during which no payments are due nor any period during which interest doesn't accrue. In other words, as soon as the parents cash the PLUS Loan check (or the money from a PLUS Loan hits your account at college), the interest clock starts ticking. If you're a parent with one of these loans and you want to maintain your credit rating, you must start paying off the PLUS Loans immediately and continue paying on a regular basis until the debt (and its interest) is completely repaid.

Perkins Loans

Federal *Perkins Loans* are loans guaranteed by the U.S. Department of Education and are available for undergraduates and graduate students. Unlike Stafford Loans, however, Federal Perkins Loans have a fixed rate of interest and are made by your college or other institution (the government gives the college the money, and the college distributes it). Federal Perkins Loans can't be subsidized by the U.S. Department of Education.

The Perkins Loan program is determined based on three factors: when you apply, the level of need as determined by your college, and the funding level of your school. Schools generally pay out Perkins Loan payments twice a year, and they usually disburse the money by check to you or by direct deposit to your student account. Typically, you have ten years to pay back any funds disbursed under the Federal Perkins Loan program, and you make your checks out directly to your school. You have a grace period of nine months after you graduate, leave school, or fall below part-time status before you must begin to repay your Perkins loan. Under certain conditions (such as active military duty), you may also defer payment for a longer period of time.

Defer or Discharge Student Loan Debt

*U*nder special circumstances, you can receive a deferment on the repayment of your federal student loans. In some circumstances, you may also be able to have your entire debt forgiven (or to use the technical term, *discharged*).

To be eligible for deferment, your loan can't be in default. If it is, contact the holder of the loan and get back on a satisfactory payment program. And you must keep making payments until you receive approval for deferment. You can't simply contact the loans office, ask for the deferment, and then stop paying.

Deferring a Stafford Loan

In some cases, you may receive a deferment of your Stafford Loan if you're unable to find full-time employment after you graduate or if you experience severe economic hardship. Many Peace Corps volunteers, for example, are eligible for Stafford Loan deferment based on economic hardship.

In some cases, you may be able to cancel your Stafford Loan debt if you qualify under one of the following specific circumstances:

- ✔ You become a full-time elementary or secondary teacher for five consecutive years in an area that serves low-income families.

- ✔ Your school closes before you can complete your program.

- ✔ Your school doesn't pay out your loan amount.

- ✔ You file for bankruptcy and the bankruptcy court decides that your student loan needs to be discharged.

- ✔ You die or become permanently disabled, making work impossible.

Putting Off Perkins Payments

You automatically get a nine-month grace period with a Perkins Loan, but you may be able to postpone repayment even longer:

- ✔ If you're unable to find work on a full-time basis, deferring your Perkins Loans repayments for up to three years may be possible.

- ✔ If you encounter severe economic hardship, you may be able to defer your repayments for up to three years.

- ✔ If you become a community service worker in such professions as law enforcement, corrections, or teaching in designated low-income areas, you may be able to defer your Perkins Loans indefinitely.

Out and out cancellation of your Perkins Loan debt is also possible. Examples of situations that may qualify for up to 100 percent of the loan being discharged include but are not limited to the following:

- ✔ Becoming a full-time special education teacher or a teacher of children with diagnosed learning disabilities at an elementary school, a secondary school, or a nonprofit institution

- ✔ Performing early intervention services for the elderly on a full-time, professional basis

- ✔ Serving as a full-time law enforcement or corrections officer

- ✔ Becoming a full-time staff member in the education division of a Head Start Program

And up to 70 percent of your Perkins Loan can be forgiven if you enlist in the AmeriCorps VISTA Program or become a Peace Corps volunteer.

Consolidate Your College Loans

A *Consolidation Loan* helps students and parents simplify the college loan repayment process. As you may guess from its name, a Consolidation Loan combines or *consolidates* various student loans that are active under your account.

Consolidation Loans are also useful whenever you want to extend your repayment duration from a maximum of 10 years allowable under the Standard Repayment Plan associated with the Stafford Loan to a maximum of 30 years allowable under the Consolidation Loan program. Besides extending the repayment period, a Consolidation Loan also offers potentially lower monthly payments, albeit for a longer overall repayment period. In addition, a Consolidation Loan can offer a way out when you've defaulted on your loan.

You can secure a Consolidation Loan from two sources:

> ✔ Direct Consolidation Loans are available directly from the U.S. government, specifically from the U.S. Department of Education.

✔ FFEL Consolidation Loans are available from a variety of participating banks, credit unions, and other lending institutions.

You can get more information about Consolidation Loan options from the Loan Origination Center's Consolidation Department at 800-577-7392 or on the Web at www.loan consolidation.ed.gov.

Find College-Based Scholarships

*C*olleges have resources to help you reduce the amount of tuition you pay. Most financial aid officers will work to help you apply for everything that may be available, but you must take the first step by asking for their help. Sometimes, asking for help is as easy as checking a box on the applicable financial aid form. Students who win more money go the extra mile by asking college financial aid officers for help and advice.

✔ **College-based scholarships:** These awards are funded by an existing endowment that's been given to the college by alumni or other interested parties. These scholarships may be need-based, merit-based, or a combination of the two.

✔ **External scholarships or grants administered by the college:** These awards are funded by an endowment held by a third party, typically outside the college. The college administers the scholarship, but you may need to apply for it separately from your general admission application.

Access State and Local Scholarships

● ●

*L*ocal scholarships tend to offer money to fewer students than their state or federal counterparts — often only one student per year. But because fewer students apply for these scholarships, you may have better chances of winning these awards than the big-money national scholarships. Talk to the following people and groups to find out about these scholarships:

> ✔ **High school guidance counselors and teachers:**
> The first person to talk to about getting free money is your high school counselor. Part of his or her job is to keep up on grants, scholarships, and loans that may be available for students from your school. Talk to your teachers about the colleges they attended and ask them for scholarship help. Even if your teacher has no specific information, he'll probably make a good reference if you decide to apply to his alma mater.

✔ **The local Parent-Teacher Association:** Some PTAs administer scholarship programs, and most have information about them. If the person you talk with at the PTA isn't helpful, ask to be given access to the national association of PTAs. The national association is busy, but it's an excellent source of contacts if you have time and patience.

✔ **Local government officials:** Some local scholarship programs operate virtually by word of mouth, so talk with your local government representatives. Drop in on the office, explain that you're looking for locally based scholarships, and ask for the appropriate person.

✔ **Chamber of Commerce:** Your local Chamber of Commerce should be able to help you identify top businesses in town. Sometimes a Chamber of Commerce offers a scholarship of its own, but this is rare. Look around to see which companies sponsor the Little League teams — companies that like to see their names on the backs of young athletes may also enjoy the prestige that comes with a scholarship presentation ceremony.

✔ **Banking community:** Scholarships are held in endowments, and someone has to administer these endowments. Talk to the manager of your bank and any other banks in the area to find out about any grants or scholarships they administer.

✔ **Places of worship:** Like service organizations, religious institutions are parts of regional, national, and international organizations. Awards may be available from any level. Ask!

Tap Organizations for Scholarships

• •

*U*ndoubtedly, you have an inkling that some organizations offer scholarships, but you may not know *which* organizations to approach. Following is some help:

- ✔ **Service and social clubs:** The Elks Club, Lions Club, Rotary Club, 4-H Club, Boy Scouts and Girl Scouts, and Greek organizations (college fraternities and sororities) are just a few examples of service and social clubs.

- ✔ **Foundations formed by corporations, groups, or individuals:** These foundations include large organizations with multiple awards, midsized organizations, and small organizations offering as few as one scholarship a year.

- ✔ **Employment or trade groups:** Professional organizations, trade unions, and military service organizations fall under this category.

Accept Work-Study Opportunities

• •

*F*ederal Work-Study is frequently offered in your financial aid package. You don't get paid much (at least
minimum wage), but Federal Work-Study jobs have three
distinct advantages:

✔ These jobs are supposed to be associated with your
field of study, and therefore, they help you gain relevant experience. Of course, a chemistry major may
get a job washing out test tubes — not necessarily
great to put on the ol' resume!

✔ Unlike an off-campus job delivering pizzas in which
you're fully taxed on your wages, income from Work-
Study jobs is eligible for deduction from your *modi-
fied adjusted gross income* (MAGI). The end result is
that Work-Study jobs let you keep more of your
hard-earned money than a regular off-campus job.

✔ Work-Study jobs are usually based around your
class time; the same isn't always true with off-
campus jobs that often interfere with your school-
work or study time.

Negotiate Better Financial Aid

After you apply to colleges and they offer you their packages, you can try to negotiate a better deal. As you do so, keep in mind that financial aid offices have a set amount of need-based and merit-based funding they can disperse, and they want to know they're getting the best possible students for the money.

Get More Need-Based Money

Getting more need-based money is generally your best option. You may qualify for more need-based funding for all sorts of reasons, including the following:

- ✔ Your circumstances have changed.
- ✔ The financial effects of certain parts of your information may not be properly understood.
- ✔ Your assessment may not take into consideration other factors.

When appealing your financial aid package based on need, make sure you provide as much documentation as possible to prove the points you're making.

Get More Merit-Based Money

Negotiating for more merit-based money is a challenge because most financial aid officers pledge almost all their money when they send out admissions offers. Still, convincing a financial aid officer that you truly should've been offered a greater entrance scholarship based on your vastly improved final marks or SAT/ACT scores is possible, depending on the school. If the officer has any discretionary budget left, your position may be reassessed. If not, the officer can certainly help you apply for other sources of funding, including departmental scholarships and external scholarships.

Refinance a Fixed-Rate Mortgage

• •

*I*f you have a fixed-rate mortgage and interest rates drop, you may want to refinance the same loan to reduce your monthly payments. The following table shows monthly payments for 15- and 30-year fixed-rate mortgages.

Interest Rate	Monthly Payments (30 yr)	Monthly Payments (15 yr)
6%	$600	$843
7%	$665	$898
8%	$733	$956
9%	$805	$1,075
10%	$878	$1,104
11%	$952	$1,137
12%	$1,029	$1,200

As you decide whether to refinance, consider the following:

- ✔ **Closing costs will add to the principal.** Every time you redo the paper, a whole assortment of people, from the lender of the title company to the appraiser, get to charge you some sort of fee. You have to add these refinancing fees into the loan principal. If you refinance $100,000 and have $3,100 added to your debt because of closing costs, you're refinancing $103,100, so your new monthly rate, instead of $665 per month, is actually $687 a month.

- ✔ **When you plan to move.** Your monthly payment may go down, but whether that saves you money in the long run depends on how long it takes to make back the money you spent for the new loan. When you start the new loan, your first payments go almost exclusively to interest. If you sell the house after two years, your loan balance is $100,930 (assuming the $3,100 in closing costs mentioned in the previous point). You save $2,832 by making lower payments for two years, but you actually owe *more* on the loan than you did in the first place. (Had you kept your original $100,000 loan amount at 9-percent interest, you'd owe $98,596 on the loan after these two years.)

Part IV

Living a Recession-Busting Life

The 5th Wave   By Rich Tennant

"...and don't tell me I'm not being frugal enough. I hired a man last week to do nothing but clip coupons!"

In this part . . .

In tough economic times, sacrifices must be made. People have to knuckle down, buckle down, tighten their belts, and pinch pennies — which all sound very bleak and discouraging. But what you really need to do is be smart about where your money goes and cut back in ways that don't feel like deprivation. With a little planning and a few changes here and there, you can keep your household humming along quite nicely, thank you very much. By following the tips in the part, you can reduce typical household expenses and still enjoy quite a few of life's luxuries.

Develop Good Shopping Habits

• •

*S*hopping is a necessity as well as a popular form of recreation, but it can often feel like a black hole on your finances. To keep your shopping trips from turning into a spending frenzy, take time to think about how you can spend more thoughtfully.

When shopping, always keep the following in mind: Reduce, reuse, and recycle. For example, don't buy overly processed, prepackaged foods. The more packaging and processing involved, the more it costs you. Reduce packaged and processed items. Prepackaged groceries generally cost at least twice as much as whole foods. For example, you can buy ready-to-heat twice-baked potatoes for approximately $1 per serving, or you can buy the ingredients to make twice-baked potatoes from scratch for less than 15¢ per serving.

Try to buy whole foods, in their natural state, whenever possible: fresh fruit, vegetables, meat, and dairy products. If you're limiting your fat intake, buy fresh eggs and discard half, or even all, of the yokes (the fat is in the yoke). This approach costs you about half as much as the reduced-fat egg substitute in a carton and is much fresher, with no additives, preservatives, or food coloring.

Reduce trash by minimizing your use of paper towels, disposable plates and cups, cloth diapers, plastic shopping bags, and so on. Instead, reuse cloth towels and diapers (they're much cheaper and much more environmentally friendly), and durable plates and cups, and take your shopping bags with you to the grocery store. Many stores credit you 5¢ per bag for bringing your own. Not only are you saving money, but you're also saving landfills. Over the course of a year, simply reusing these items can save you tens of dollars. Just think of how many other items this concept could apply to.

Reduce the number of items you purchase by sharing with, or renting from, others. For example, if you like to garden, a rototiller comes in handy once or twice a year. Instead of buying a rototiller, consider borrowing one from a neighbor or renting one.

See through the Gimmicks Grocery Stores Use

• •

Grocery stores spend money to learn how to fool you into spending more in their store. Whether they're enticing you into the store in the first place with sale items or convincing you to buy more expensive items, be aware of some of these tactics:

- ✔ **The aisle switcheroo:** If you shop at a particular store regularly, you know where everything you buy is located in each aisle. Without realizing it, you've developed a form of tunnel vision and don't really see anything except what you need. When the store rearranges the aisles or moves items from one position on a shelf to another, you have to look around and actually focus on each aisle and every shelf. By losing your tunnel vision for a time, the possibility of something new catching your eye increases dramatically, and consequently your impulse purchases increase, too.

- ✔ **The store's layout:** Most grocery stores have the same general floor plan — they keep produce, bread, dairy, and meat products along the edges of the store or up against the walls. By putting commonly purchased items against the farthest wall or way off in a back corner, customers have to walk past numerous displays and shelves full of goodies.

Shop the edges of the store to save considerably on your grocery bill. Added benefit: The perimeter carries the healthiest items in the store. Your waistline — and your budget — will be healthier.

✓ **The loss leaders:** Stores advertise products for essentially zero profit to entice new customers into the store for the drastically reduced item. They're willing to take a loss on selected items because they plan to recoup their loss through higher sales in general due to the increased traffic. The key to taking advantage of these so-called *loss leaders* without letting loss leaders take advantage of you is to not give in to temptation.

Check the expiration date on any loss leader purchases. Often these items are near their expiration date and the store is trying to clear them off its shelves.

✓ **Shelf arrangements:** If you want to find the best values on the grocery store shelves, look high on the top shelves or bend down and look at the bottom shelf. The brand-name and higher-priced products (as well as products designed to entice children) are located at eye level, while the generic, store brand, and lower-priced items are in the more awkward places to see.

Use Coupons Wisely

• •

*T*he key to effective coupon use is to be organized about the process. Every coupon you need but can't easily locate is cash slipping through your fingers. Try those little wallet-shaped coupon organizers you can slip into your purse or pocket to keep your coupons organized by category. Once a month go through your coupon organizer to check for expired coupons.

To make the most of your coupon savings, follow these suggestions:

✔ Look for double- and triple-coupon deals.

✔ Look for coupons for items that are already on sale or that are deeply discounted.

✔ Don't assume you get the best deal with the coupon; store brands can still be cheaper.

✔ Don't plan your shopping list around the manufacturer's coupons you've collected; instead make your regular shopping list first, and then go to your coupon wallet and see whether you have current coupons for the items you're buying.

✔ When shopping online, look for online coupon codes to save on the purchase price or on shipping and handling charges; just type the name of the site you're shopping at and **coupons** into your favorite search engine to see what you find.

Target Seasonal Grocery Sales

• •

*I*n addition to in-store sales and offers, many food items go on sale at regular times from year to year. For example, March is National Frozen Food Month in the United States, and to celebrate this prestigious event, most grocery stores offer significant discounts on frozen foods during the month of March. Throughout the rest of the year, other food items are seasonally offered at discounts. The lower prices usually reflect what's currently growing at local farms.

The following list includes food items you can find on sale or at the lowest prices each month of the year:

- ✔ **January:** Turkey, apples, grapefruit, oranges, and pears
- ✔ **February:** Post–Valentine's Day candy and chocolates
- ✔ **March:** Frozen vegetables, meats, breakfast items, and TV dinners
- ✔ **April:** Eggs, broccoli, and cauliflower
- ✔ **May:** Soda, hot dogs, hamburgers, buns, asparagus, and pineapple

- **June:** Dairy products and tomatoes
- **July:** Strawberries, raspberries, blueberries, corn, cherries, squash, watermelons, cantaloupes, tomatoes, plums, peaches, and nectarines
- **August:** Squash, green peppers, salad fixings, berries, apples, melons, peaches, apricots, and fresh fish
- **September:** Apples, broccoli, cauliflower, and canned goods
- **October:** Pumpkins, cranberries, grapes, oranges, sweet potatoes, and yams
- **November:** Turkey, sweet potatoes, yams, and post-Halloween bags of candy
- **December:** Oranges, apples, and grapefruit

Plan Your Meals Economically

$\mathcal{W}$hether you're feeding yourself or a family, meal-times present a challenge when you want to save money without sacrificing your favorites. You want healthy, tasty menus that everyone will enjoy and that won't send your budget into cardiac arrest.

Find a Breakfast You and Your Wallet Will Love

With $5 boxes of cereal that are gone in a day, breakfast bars not much cheaper, and egg prices going up and up, breakfast can be one of the most expensive meals of the day. Here are ways to save:

✔ **Make homemade versions of frequently purchased breakfast items, such as frozen waffles or instant oatmeal.** For example, make instant oatmeal at home by briefly whirling oats in the blender or food processor. Then just stir in boiling water as you normally would for instant oats.

✔ **Keep a list of favorite breakfast ideas.** Examples of quick, healthy, and inexpensive options include

- **Breakfast shakes or smoothies:** Blend a few ice cubes with your choice of fresh or generic canned fruits and juice.

- **Fresh or canned fruit:** Whole, sliced, or stewed.

- **Omelets:** Use up leftover pieces of meat, vegetables, and cheese to keep omelets inexpensive.

- **Bagels:** Serve toasted and spread with butter; or spread with generic cream cheese. Sliced strawberries, when they're in season, and generic cream cheese on bagels is an almost decadent breakfast treat. Look for sales on bagels and stock up. They keep for weeks in the freezer.

- **Mule food:** Stir together uncooked rolled oats, raisins, and nuts. Serve cold with milk and your choice of sweetener (honey, sugar, brown sugar, maple syrup, vanilla, fruit juice, almond extract); or just stir the "mule food" into your favorite flavored yogurt. Make this treat in bulk and store in an air-tight container for a great substitute for brand-name boxed granola.

- **Use leftovers:** Cold pizza makes a nice break-fast. So does a cheese enchilada and vegetar-ian lasagna.

Brown-Bag It in Style

Bringing homemade lunch items with you to work or school is a surefire way to save money every day during the week. But who says a packed lunch has to be PB&J and pudding snacks in a paper bag? Turn a bagged lunch into something special and *still* save a boatload of money every week with these tips:

- ✓ **Be creative with your menu:** Vary your menu from day to day to keep your palate happy. Even if you like the routine of a sandwich every day, be creative with the side dish.

- ✓ **Spice it up:** Add fresh herbs (fresh basil sprinkled over leftover pasta, for example) or fancier condiments (horseradish for the roast beef sandwich).

- ✓ **Go for the extraordinary:** Instead of run-of-the-mill cheese cubes, pack a variety of cheeses (cheddar, parmesan, and brie, for example) with a couple slices of shaved ham, a few olives, some fruit, and crackers. Trade up the white bread for crusty rolls or baguettes. Roll the grapes in sugar, or take along a small container of chocolate sauce for dipping your fruit.

- ✓ **Set your table:** You may not be able to re-create the ambience of a five-star restaurant in your office or cafeteria, but you can make lunchtime more enjoyable by using a linen napkin, a real plate (or reasonable facsimile), and genuine flatware. Keep these items in your office if transporting them is a hassle.

- ✓ **Take your time:** Meals are meant to be savored, even when you have only 15 minutes in which to eat. So turn off the phone, turn away from the computer, and enjoy your lunch.

Save on Scrumptious Dinners

Living well involves setting priorities; if yours include being healthy and omitting needless spending, you know that dinnertime makes it difficult to stay on track. The following list offers a few ideas to help you save time and money and still end up with a great dinner:

- ✔ **Serve breakfast for dinner:** Bacon and eggs may be a fairly expensive breakfast to serve the family, but it's a very cheap meal compared to most dinner menus. For a healthier alternative, use turkey bacon or sausage, or try a veggie-filled frittata. Making an occasional breakfast for dinner can be a real treat.

- ✔ **Focus on the sides:** If you're not a vegetarian, think of meat as a side dish rather than the main course. A small serving of chicken with a large tossed salad and a generous serving of steamed vegetables or rice is better for you and can save tremendously compared to having the meat be the largest item on your dinner plate.

- ✔ **Serve salad.** A chef salad, for example, includes a little meat and a lot of vegetables, and it's even better and less expensive if the vegetables are in season.

Save on Snacks

Kids thrive on the classic after-school snack, but adults are often in need of a healthy pick-me-up as well. Give these healthy, frugal snack options a try:

- **Crackers with toppings:** Spread peanut butter or cream cheese on a cracker, or top with sliced meats and cheeses.

- **Assorted cheeses:** Serve cubed or sliced cheeses alone or with apples, crackers, celery, or meats.

- **Popcorn:** Sprinkle popcorn with flavored salt or Parmesan cheese for a nice change of pace.

- **Fresh fruit in season:** Limit this healthy afternoon snack to one piece of fruit per person or the cost can quickly become prohibitive.

- **Cut-up veggies:** Keeping cut-up celery, carrots, cauliflower, broccoli, or other veggies on hand and easily accessible in the fridge makes healthy snacking a piece of cake or, in this case, a piece of vegetable.

- **Cinnamon toast:** Toast the bread, spread the butter, sprinkle on a bit of sugar and cinnamon, and you're good to go.

- **Mock ice cream sandwich:** Put 2 tablespoons of frozen whipped topping between two chocolate graham crackers, wrap it in wax paper, and freeze for a half hour. It tastes just like an ice cream sandwich, but it's healthier (especially if you use lowfat whipped topping) and less expensive.

Stretch One Meal into Two (Or More)

• •

*T*ossing a glob of warmed-up old noodles onto a plate doesn't entice many appetites. But if you use a little creativity, leftovers can be fun, tasty, inexpensive meal starters. By camouflaging the leftovers from meal to meal, even your pickiest eaters will have trouble recognizing the roasted chicken from dinner two nights ago in today's pasta salad luncheon.

Make a Leftover Buffet

Plan one meal each week that uses up the assorted leftovers accumulating on the refrigerator shelves. It's like getting a free meal every week.

After accumulating about half a dozen containers of leftovers, reheat them in the microwave and portion out a little bit of everything onto each person's plate. Generally, nobody ends up with more than a spoonful or two of any one item, but the variety of items gives it the look of a full plate after you've gone through a buffet line at a party: a dab of lasagna, a slice of roasted chicken, half a black bean enchilada, a forkful of several types of salad. Toss some crackers, sliced cheese, and fresh cut-up veggies into the mix, and you have an easy dinner that the whole family enjoys.

Sandwich Your Leftovers into Savings

A favorite use for leftovers is to make sandwiches for lunch or dinner. Whether it's leftover roast beef made into French dips, or sliced meatloaf with mayo and ketchup, or an open-faced turkey sandwich smothered in gravy, your family will love the results. Rolling leftover meats and veggies into a cold, flour tortilla with a bit of cream cheese and a pickle is also a delicious way to add some variety to the typical sandwich presentation.

Stretch the Bird

Chicken and turkey are dreams come true if you want to stretch one meal into several others. For a family of four, you can usually stretch at least three meals from each chicken purchase: a roast chicken dinner meal consisting of the drumsticks, thighs, and wings; a casserole, stir-fry, or skillet meal prepared with the cut breast meat roasted the night before; and a hearty, homemade chicken soup made from any leftover meat and bones. Each time you buy a chicken, plan ahead for the three chicken meals.

Turkeys, because of their size, can yield even more meals. Round one can be a turkey dinner with all the trimmings. Then from the leftovers, create casseroles, sandwiches, stir-fry, pot pies, you name it. After you pick the bones clean of meat, make a turkey broth (follow the same recipe to make a chicken broth):

1. Place the carcass in a 6-quart saucepan.

2. Add 2 carrots and 2 stalks of celery cut into 1-inch pieces and one onion, peeled and whole.

3. Fill the pot with enough water to cover by 1 inch. Bring to a boil over high heat.

4. Lower heat to a simmer and cook for 1½ hours.

5. When cooled to room temperature, remove and discard the carcass and vegetables.

6. Pour the liquid though a fine strainer. Season the broth with salt and black pepper to taste.

Make your own mixes

For the sake of convenience, you probably buy premade and prepackaged products (such as salad dressing, taco seasoning, and cookie and cake mixes). Going homemade is not only cheaper, but also considerably healthier. You can choose which ingredients to use, and you also know that no flavorings, colorings, or preservatives are added.

Find recipes for convenience items by looking at the ingredient lists on the package and getting a good idea of what to use, browsing through all-purpose cookbooks and cooking-related books at the library, and logging on to www.recipesource.com/misc/mixes or www.frugalitynetwork.com/frugalrecipes.mixes.html.

Save on Baby Food

*F*rugal hardly seems like a word to use in the same sentence as "baby food," which can really take a bite out of the ol' budget. But buying the expensive prepackaged baby foods isn't the only way to feed baby. You have numerous less expensive (and more healthful) options:

- ✔ **Breastfeed:** The least expensive baby food available is the mother's milk: it's free. If you can breastfeed your little one, you save a bundle compared to buying formula, and you're also providing your baby with the best possible nutrition. Even if you're working full time outside the home, breastfeeding is still an option. For breastfeeding tips, contact a local breastfeeding organization such as La Leche League (www.lalecheleague.org), or ask your local hospital or doctor's office to recommend a certified lactation consultant.

- ✔ **Process your own baby food:** Serve your baby tiny servings — well-processed in the blender or food processor first — of most anything the family is already eating: potatoes, carrots, peas, or even homemade chicken soup. Take care to leave out spices and any additives in baby's portion.

   Prepare a large batch of baby food at one time so you don't need to do it at every meal. For example, cook and puree a big bunch of carrots, freeze the puree in ice cube trays, pop out the frozen food cubes, and place in labeled zip-top freezer bags. When your baby's ready to eat, just take out a frozen carrot cube, thaw it, warm slightly, and dinner is served.

✔ **If you buy premade baby food, buy the largest jars available.** The little bitty jars may be meal-sized for baby's tiny appetite, but they're expensive too. When you open a large jar, spoon out a small portion onto a plate or bowl, and then cover the jar and refrigerate it. The large jar of food lasts for about two meals this way, rather than just one.

✔ **Dilute regular juice to give to baby:** The special baby juice at the grocery store is really nothing more than diluted regular juice. Just buy regular 100-percent juice in frozen concentrate form (with no additives or sweeteners), but then add twice the amount of water (or more) recommended when you're reconstituting the juice.

Cook Up Money Savings

*E*ating out often can zap your budget, but busy sched-ules make it difficult to find the time to fix healthy, tasty, and economical home-cooked meals. The suggestions here can help.

Cook in Bulk

The idea of cooking in bulk and freezing the premade meals puts off many people. They hear terms referring to *monthly* cooking or *30-day* cooking, and they roll their eyes. But think of it more as a concept. If you don't have the freezer space, the energy, or organizational where-withal for a full month of cooking in one pop, try twice-a-month, or even once-a-week. Or just double and triple recipes as you prepare them.

Here's how bulk cooking works: When you make chili, make enough for three meals. Eat one tonight, and then package the extra in labeled freezer bags. You now have two meals ready to go in just minutes for those nights when you're in a hurry. Just pop the freezer bag in the microwave or pour the thawed chili into a pan on the stovetop, toss together a green salad, and dinner is served.

For additional savings, plan your bulk-cooking sessions around the supermarket's sales. Suppose, for example, that your grocery store has whole fryers on sale. You buy the maximum number of fryers the store allows (four in this example) and do a chicken mini-session: You cut up the fryers, and then prepare and freeze the following meals:

- ✔ **Two or three meals' worth of marinated thighs and drumsticks in plastic freezer bags.** The chicken marinates while it's frozen and also while it thaws. You can use homemade Italian-style salad dressing for a marinade or generic or store-brand dressing. To serve, thaw completely, pour off the marinade, and then cook the chicken pieces on the barbecue or under the oven broiler.

- ✔ **Two meals of chicken cacciatore.** A tasty freeze-ahead version consists of sliced chicken breast, a jar of spaghetti sauce, stewed tomatoes, and some sautéed onions and green pepper strips. Thaw the cacciatore and serve it over pasta or rice.

- ✔ **Several meals' worth of cooked chicken.** Cut the chicken into medium-sized chunks to use in skillet meals or casseroles. Having freezer bags with pre-cooked and frozen chicken pieces makes later meal preparation a snap.

- ✔ **A large pot of homemade chicken noodle soup.** Soup is usually good for at least two meals, maybe more, depending on how hungry the troops are when they're ready to eat.

Be sure to vary your menus to keep your family happy. Even when foods are dressed differently, few people like the same thing night after night. Just because you've prepared all these chicken-based meals doesn't mean you have to serve them one day after another.

To ensure your meals are thawed and ready to heat up at dinner time, plan your dinners two days in advance. Most frozen casseroles, for example, take about 48 hours to thaw.

Use a Slow Cooker

A slow cooker is both convenient and a money saver. When you come home at dinnertime, dinner's nearly done, eliminating the temptation to run out for something quick (and usually less healthy and definitely more expensive). But slow cookers can save you money in other ways:

- ✔ You can cook larger meals, providing leftovers and possibly a second meal from one cooking time.

- ✔ You can buy tougher (and less expensive) cuts of meat because the slow cooker acts as a tenderizer.

- ✔ Meat shrinks less when cooked in the slow cooker and doesn't dry out. Also, flavors have time to develop while your meal cooks all day.

- ✔ A slow cooker doesn't use as much electricity as an oven, nor does it heat up the kitchen nearly as much as the stovetop or oven, so it's a perfect hot-weather cooking appliance.

- ✔ A slow cooker frees up oven and stovetop space during a large cooking session for the freezer.

- ✔ Tofu, an inexpensive meat substitute, tastes better cooked in a slow cooker because it has time to soak up the flavors of the broth, spices, and other ingredients.

A pressure cooker has many benefits similar to the slow cooker and is also much faster. If you don't have all day for your meal to simmer on the counter, the pressure cooker is a great option.

Can It!

• •

*H*ome-canning is a safe and economical way to preserve high-quality food. If you love fresh ingredients, like working in the kitchen, and want to create
gourmet-quality specialty foods for less than you'd spend
in the gourmet aisle of a supermarket, you can save
money and eat well with a little effort. The money savings
comes from two factors:

✔ With a well-stocked pantry of canned produce, you
   can eliminate or significantly reduce having to buy
   expensive alternatives.

✔ The best produce for canning is fresh, fresh, fresh.
   You're lucky if you grow your own fruit or veggies,
   or have a friend who shares hers with you. Or you
   can buy in bulk from farmers markets when the produce is in season. Some growers offer a "pick your
   own" option, which is even cheaper yet.

Types of Canning

Although you may hear of many canning methods, only
two are approved by the United States Department of
Agriculture (USDA):

✓ **Water-bath canning:** This method uses a large kettle of boiling water. Filled jars are submerged in the water and heated to an internal temperature of 212 degrees Fahrenheit for a specific period of time. Use this method for processing high-acid foods, such as fruit, items made from fruit, pickles, pickled food, and tomatoes.

✓ **Pressure canning:** Pressure canning uses a large kettle that produces steam in a locked compartment. The filled jars in the kettle reach an internal temperature of 240 degrees Fahrenheit under a specific pressure (stated in pounds) that's measured with a dial gauge or weighted gauge on the pressure-canner cover. Use a pressure canner for processing vegetables and other low-acid foods, such as meat, poultry, and fish.

In both of these methods, your filled jars of food are heated to a high temperature that destroys microorganisms and produces a vacuum seal. Produce a safe product by using the correct method for the food type, following the recipe instructions to the letter, and completing each processing step.

Canning with Success

Follow these tips for achieving success as a home canner:

✓ Start with the freshest, best products available.

✓ Know the rules and techniques for your canning or preserving method.

✓ Work in short sessions to prevent fatigue and potential mistakes.

✔ Stay up-to-date on new or revised guidelines for your preserving method.

✔ Use the correct processing method and processing time to destroy microorganisms.

✔ Know the elevation you're working at.

✔ Put together a plan before you start your preserving session.

Grow your own produce

Whether you have a large or small yard (or no yard at all), you can grow a garden that drastically cuts down your produce bill five months out of the year. Here's how:

✔ Pick a prime location. The garden should get six to eight hours of sun a day and be in close proximity to both your house and the water supply. Or try container gardening, which works wonders on small decks and patios.

✔ Decide what veggies to grow: Start with about four or five easy-to-grow varieties of vegetables (such as tomatoes, bush beans, lettuce, cucumbers, and zucchini) — whatever your family eats regularly and works well with your soil and climate conditions. For specifics about regional growing recommendations for your area, consult a local home and garden center or ask your friendly gardening neighbors what they suggest.

✔ Weed and enjoy!

Other Ways to Save in the Kitchen

*E*very tip helps when you're trying to save money in the kitchen, so here's a list of easy ideas to help cut the cost of family meals.

- Keep lettuce fresh longer by rinsing and drying it thoroughly. (Use a salad spinner, if available.) Then cut the lettuce into salad-size pieces (use a lettuce knife to reduce the risk of bruising), place in a zip-top bag, try to get all the excess air out of the bag, and then store the bag of lettuce in the refrigerator. Each time you use some of the lettuce, press the air out again. Lettuce keeps for as long as a week this way if it's dry before you place it in the bag.

- Don't rinse produce until you're going to use it; otherwise, it can mold and get slimy faster.

- Save the bits and pieces of leftover pie crust in a zip-top bag in the freezer. When you have enough in the bag, you can make another pie crust or two from the thawed pieces.

- Use half the amount of meat called for in the recipe when making a casserole or skillet meal, and then add inexpensive vegetables or pasta to fill in for the missing meat.

✔ Stretch ground beef in hamburgers, meatloaves, and meatballs by stirring in cut-up bread crusts, oat-meal, homemade bread crumbs, cracker crumbs, or plain cereals. This is a great way to use up stale crackers.

✔ Use turkey hot dogs instead of beef or pork. Turkey is often half the price.

✔ Buy blocks of cheese when they're on sale, grate, and place in a large zip-top freezer bag. Use it as needed. If the cheese clumps together in the freezer, bang the bag against the kitchen counter to loosen.

✔ Buy eggs when they're on sale and freeze for later use in baking, omelets, and scrambled eggs. Don't freeze the eggs whole; crack each egg into a section of a clean plastic ice cube tray. When frozen, remove the egg cubes from the tray and package in a large zip-top freezer bag. Use as needed. The thawed out eggs should be used quickly — they're very perishable.

✔ Fill the oven with baking potatoes when you have to heat it up to bake a few potatoes for dinner. Eat tonight's potatoes, cool the leftover ones, and freeze in zip-top bags. For a quick and inexpensive meal or side dish, reheat the frozen potatoes in the microwave.

#69

Save on Salon Expenses

. . . .

*W*hen you're trying to be a conscientious consumer, salon visits pose a dilemma. On the one hand, visiting a stylist once every six weeks is a luxury you can surely do without. On the other hand, looking and feeling good is darn near priceless. The key is to find a balance that lets you have your cake and eat it to. Here are some ideas:

- Negotiate services with your stylist.

- Extend time between visits.

- Go to a discount salon or a beauty college between visits with your regular stylist.

- Trim your own bangs to extend the life of your style between salon visits.

- Cut your kids' hair yourself rather than taking them to the salon. They don't need the extra pampering just yet.

Expand Your Wardrobe

Dressing well doesn't have to equal dressing expensively. A great place to find clothing is at thrift stores and garage sales. Even if your family's wardrobe consists of almost nothing but secondhand clothing, you can all still look great. The following sections suggest other ways to expand your child's wardrobe without decimating your budget.

 A wardrobe of basic colors and simple styles makes mix-and-match dressing practical, easy, and much less expensive than buying outfits made of pieces that can only be worn with each other.

Make the Most of Hand-Me-Downs

Using hand-me-downs is a wonderful way to save money and recycle still serviceable clothing items. If you have friends and family with kids slightly older than yours, ask them to save their children's outgrown clothing for you. Most parents are happy to save clothes for a friend, but may not know who's interested in their hand-me-downs.

Exchange Clothing

Start a regular group clothing exchange throughout the year. Here's how it works: Everyone brings her family's outgrown or discarded clothing to someone's home, displays it on a table, and then sorts through everyone else's castoffs to find clothing for her own family. At the end of the exchange, the leftovers are boxed up and donated to a thrift store.

Shop Seasonally and Plan Ahead

At the end of each season, you can find huge savings on seasonal clothing items. The best *selection* of clothes is usually at the beginning of the season, but the best *bargains* are at the end. Watch for seasonal sales at local stores, where you can stock up on items you'll use throughout the year.

If you're buying for your kids and you see an excellent price, stock up on larger sizes. Your kids can grow into them as time passes.

Save on School Clothes

Wait until the school year begins to buy the bulk of your kids' school clothing, so they can see what's in style and what's out of fashion. Waiting until after school starts allows you to take advantage of clearance sale prices at department stores, thrift stores, and secondhand shops.

If you want to dress your kids in designer duds for discount prices, look online at auction sites such as
www.ebay.com. You can also score brand-name clothing
and accessories at consignment stores.

Modify your driving techniques

These driving techniques can help you save fuel:

✔ Arrange your car seat as comfortably as possible.

✔ Start and accelerate slowly and smoothly.

✔ Obey the speed limits, especially in city traffic.

✔ Try to stay in your lane.

✔ Set a steady pace.

✔ Build up speed slowly before you get to a hill.

✔ If you have a manual transmission, shift into higher gears as soon
as possible.

Remove Stains from Clothing

*H*ere are some ideas to try for some common stubborn stains:

- ✔ **Baby formula: Apply stick stain remover as soon as possible.** Let it sit overnight, and then launder as usual. If the stain persists, soak overnight in a solution of non-chlorine bleach mixed with warm water (use ¼ scoop bleach per gallon of water). Launder again.

- ✔ **Blood: Rinse immediately with cool water.** Hot water sets the stain and makes it harder to remove. Dab hydrogen peroxide on white fabrics. If the stain persists, soak overnight in a solution of non-chlorine bleach and warm water.

- ✔ **Chocolate: Rinse immediately with cold water.** If the stain persists, soak overnight in a solution of non-chlorine bleach and warm water.

- ✔ **Grass: Apply a stick stain remover immediately.** Let sit overnight. Wash as usual. Or pretreat overnight in non-chlorine bleach mixed with water.

- ✔ **Gravy: Rinse thoroughly in cold water as soon as possible.** If the spot is dry, soak it in cold water for several hours. If the stain remains, apply liquid dishwashing detergent directly to the stain. Squeeze the detergent into the fabric so it gets between the fibers. Let sit overnight. Rinse thoroughly in cold water, and then wash as usual.

✔ **Ink: Apply stick stain remover as soon as possible.** Gently work stain remover into the fabric. Let it sit for several hours before washing. Launder in cold water.

✔ **Juice: Pretreat with liquid dishwashing detergent or stick stain remover.** Wash as usual in hot water. Repeat pretreatment and laundering if necessary.

✔ **Ketchup: Rinse the stain in cold water immediately.** Soak the garment in cold water for several hours. Launder in cold water. If the stain remains, use stick stain remover, let sit overnight, and launder again.

Reconstruct Your Clothes

• •

*R*econstructing clothing is the practice of creating new clothes from existing garments. Some examples of this include

- Adding a simple hood to a jacket
- Cutting the sleeves off a T-shirt
- Turning your sheets into a skirt
- Cropping a sweater
- Creating a couture evening gown from an old duvet cover

When it comes to saving cash, reusing and reconstructing clothes just can't be beat.

Types of Reconstruction

People with all levels of sewing skill can reconstruct clothes. Creative types who don't like to use patterns excel at this, and it's a fun way to make old or out-of-style clothing new again.

Mind-altering alterations

Sometimes clothing is just fine in its present form, but it needs a little something. Maybe you want to add a little pizzazz and individuality to your garment, or maybe you want to fix a poor fit, hide stains, or spruce up a worn 'n' torn favorite.

Lots of clothing is well-made and practical. But it can also be boring and can look exactly like every other piece that was mass-produced from the same factory! Some less intense reconstruction techniques serve to elevate your ho-hum hoodie to a truly unique piece of self-expression:

- ✔ Sewing a hem with contrasting color thread
- ✔ Taking in a seam with the seam placed externally
- ✔ Decorative patching on wear 'n' tear
- ✔ Decorative stitching on patches and hems
- ✔ Decorative painting over stains

These techniques are exciting for all levels of skill and creativity. And they're perfect for those pieces that you're on the fence about banishing from your closet! Plus you have lots of no-sew options with this method.

Clothing for cloth

What do you do when your heart can't let go of a piece, but you can't bear to see it hang wastefully in the storage closet? Dismantle the existing garment, creating flat fabric that you can salvage and incorporate into other things, like a quilt. You may choose to do this for a variety of reasons:

- ✔ The fabric is gorgeous but the garment is horrible

- ✔ The garment shape can't be maintained because of style or other pitfalls

- ✔ The garment is excessively large

- ✔ The fabric is an *oh so precious* vintage

- ✔ The fabric is of high quality, such as silk

- ✔ The fabric has extensive beadwork or other embellishments that you want to save

- ✔ The garment has sentimental significance, but the style and fit aren't for you

Find Fun in Community Resources

● ●

*B*efore you plunk down your hard-earned money to join a gym or for various types of entertainment and activities, consider what your community has to offer — usually at little or no cost!

- ✔ Community swimming pools
- ✔ Gymnasium or exercise classes
- ✔ Community center
- ✔ Local parks or jogging trails
- ✔ County libraries
- ✔ Museums and galleries
- ✔ Concerts
- ✔ Festivals

Have Fun in Your Own Backyard and Beyond

• •

*T*he family activities highlighted here are not only fun and cost next to nothing, but they also help build family relationships because you spend time together pursuing enjoyable pastimes.

Take a Family Field Trip

A meaningful family field trip can be simple, like taking a leisurely walk down a local nature trail and watching a pair of red squirrels do aerial acrobatics. Or extend the field trip and follow the path of Lewis and Clark across the United States for a long — but relatively inexpensive — educational family vacation. Even camping in your own backyard can be an adventure of sorts. Here are the rules:

✔ **Choose an event the entire family enjoys.** The weekly "What's Happening?" section of the newspaper and monthly issues of regional parenting magazines — often available for free in libraries and bookstores — provide a never-ending variety of activities that appeal to the entire family, from preschoolers to adults. Also, your local library may offer classes, readings, and live performances for kids. Check your library's bulletin board for notices about family-friendly activities and attractions.

✔ **Do a little pretrip planning.** A little advance planning can make for a more enjoyable — and less expensive — trip. Before you leave home, pack some inexpensive snack supplies and drink bottles, confirm driving directions, check on admission prices, and check your destination's Web site for any "online only" coupons (this would also be a good time to check for unanticipated park closures or hour changes).

Discover the Games People Play

Family games can be enjoyed whenever you want some inexpensive entertainment and time together. Institute a family game night.

If you don't have a closet full of board games, you can acquire them inexpensively at garage sales and thrift stores. If someone asks what to get you or your family for a gift at the holidays, suggest a board game.

Board games aren't the only family-friendly games to play on a family game night. Do you remember Charades? How about Spoons? Twenty Questions? Hide the Thimble? Spotlight Tag? Rummy? Crazy Eights? Delve into the recesses of your mind and try to remember the games you played as a kid. The games may be old to you, but they're *new* to your kids!

Plan a Movie Night

Going out to a movie can be real treat — and, given the price of tickets nowadays, even matinees can break the bank. But even if heading to the Cineplex is no longer within your budget, you don't have to forego the enjoyment of watching films. Rent a video, pop some corn, and invite the kids to a movie night.

Check out churches and libraries where you can often borrow movies for free. If you have cable television, keep your eye on the movie listings. You can record movies early in the week to watch on the weekends. Movies recorded from the television are not only free, but they also save you a drive to the video store or library.

Save for a Family Vacation

*F*inding money in the family's budget for a trip — large or small — can be challenging but not impossible. If you cut back on smaller activities during the year, you can pocket the money you save and put it into your vacation fund. Here are some ideas for saving a little here and a little there to fund a family getaway:

- Watch movies on television.
- Save all your loose change in a jar.
- Have a yard sale.
- Sell some clothing at a consignment store.
- Babysit or work a part-time job during the school year.
- Tally up the money you save by using coupons at the grocery store each week and put that amount in a vacation fund.

Travel on a Few Dollars a Day

All travel seems to have the same basic expenses: food, accommodations, and fun activities. What you spend on these things can amount to a lot or a little. The difference depends on where you go, how you get there, and what you do when you get there.

Choose Less-Expensive Travel Times

If possible, take your vacation during off times. The months of May and September (in the Northern Hemisphere) are especially good times to travel because they're not as hot as July or August, they're not prime tourist season, and the weather is usually nice. Many resorts offer a schedule of rates, showing their peak and off-seasons. To maximize your money and enjoyment of available perks, make your reservation for the week just before the peak time starts or right after it ends.

Be aware that "off times" in your area may not be "off times" at your destination. Holidays and regular breaks from school (winter and spring break, summer vacation from school) are also usually expensive times for travel.

Book Affordable Accommodations

Accommodations are often one of the most expensive parts of any vacation. But less-expensive alternatives exist:

- ✔ **Camping:** If you have a tent or a trailer, you can often pull into a campground almost anywhere and find a spot to sleep for about $40 per night for the whole family.

- ✔ **Hotels:** If you plan to stay at a hotel, be sure to ask about special prices or seasonal deals when you call to make a reservation. Depending on when you're traveling, ask about Sunday nights, which are often slow and hotels offer cheaper rates to encourage customers to stay.

  Call during the day when the office staff are on duty. They're more likely to know what special discounts or rates the hotel is offering.

- ✔ **Home swaps:** Working out a house swap with friends or family who live in different cities or countries can be a great way to get a vacation for no more than the cost of airfare and food. For more information on house swapping, visit www.homelink.org or do a Web search for house swapping.

- ✔ **Timeshares:** If you travel often, buying the right to use a condo or home during particular weeks of the year can be a good money-saving idea in the long run. (***Remember:*** If you buy a timeshare from the owner instead of from the resort or developer, you save substantially.)

Traveling in a group can cut accommodation costs. Take a vacation with some other families or your in-laws. Rent a big house at the ocean or stay in a mountain lodge and have everyone split the cost.

Eat Well for Less

Don't eat all your meals in restaurants. Here are some ideas for restaurant alternatives:

- ✔ If your hotel or motel offers a free breakfast, take full advantage of it.

- ✔ Eat a huge breakfast, and then have a light lunch of fruit and cheese or an energy bar.

- ✔ Visit a local supermarket and pick up the ingredients for a picnic. Make your own sandwiches, grab a bag of chips, and buy whatever soda is on sale.

- ✔ Stay hydrated. Thirst can be mistaken for hunger, and getting something to drink is usually a lot cheaper (think water fountain) than getting something to eat.

- ✔ Carry snacks with you so you're not tempted to buy pricey snacks to satisfy your hunger pangs.

You'll likely want to eat in restaurants at least part of the time — you're on vacation, after all. Plan your main meal around lunchtime. Restaurants' lunch menus are similar to dinner menus, but the cost is greatly reduced.

Plan for Fun, Not Flash

One of the best ways to save money on vacation is to under-plan activities. You don't have to see *everything*. Three major activities per area or per city is a good average. Or no more than two major activities per day. Spend the rest of your time just hanging out and wandering around.

Look into the cheap — or free! — activities your destination offers: hiking, walking on the beach, making sand castles, having a campfire, star-gazing, fishing, crabbing, or swimming.

Save on Phone Bills

● ●

Keeping in touch by phone is an expensive proposition, so cutting back on the monthly phone bill is a welcome relief to many pocketbooks:

- Check your phone bill and make sure you're not paying for extra services you never use or don't need. If you have an answering machine, you probably don't need voice mail from the phone company. If you have voice mail but no answering machine, consider buying one. Owning your own machine is less expensive over time than paying monthly fees for voice mail.

- Check to see whether your phone company offers a flat rate or a measured service plan that can save you money based on how often you call or on the times and days you usually use the phone.

- Use a cellphone for long-distance calls. (Most plans charge a flat fee a set number of minutes that you can use for both local and long-distance calls.) If you use your landline for long-distance calls, make them in the evenings and on weekends, when rates are usually lower. If you make a lot of long-distance calls, find a calling plan that suits the amount of calls you make.

✔ Look into Internet phone services that offer free or reduced plans. For example, if you (and the person you want to call) have webcams, you can use Skype (www.skype.com) to make free video calls anywhere in the world.

✔ To save money on cellphone bills, look for plans that offer minutes the entire family can share or that offer free minutes if you call in-network; instead of getting a phone for each child, get a single phone your children can share; examine your monthly bill to see how you're using your minutes and, if you consistently have minutes left over, ask about dropping to a cheaper plan.

✔ Investigate package deals. Getting phone, Internet, and TV service from one provider can often save you money.

✔ Send an e-mail (it's free) or rediscover the joys of letter writing. Sending cards and letters via the U.S. Postal Service doesn't have to cost much more than the price of a first-class stamp if you watch for specials on stationery while you're shopping.

Stay Cool on the Cheap

* *

*F*ollowing are some ways to stay cool, even when it's hot outside:

- **To drop your cooling (and heating) bills dramatically, add insulation to your home.** First insulate your attic floor, and then when time and money allow, add insulation to your basement, exterior walls, floors, and crawl spaces (in that order).

- **Improve attic ventilation:** Adequate ventilation under the eaves allows cooler air to enter and circulate throughout the attic. If you don't have a permanent exhaust fan, you can set a box fan with the air flow pointed outward to pull the hot air out of the house.

- **Shade your house from the sun:** If your house isn't shaded by trees, install awnings over any windows that are exposed to direct sun during the day. Many awnings are removable and adjustable, so you aren't stuck with them when you don't need them.

- **Cover your windows:** Windows are a major source of heat during the summer. Reduce the heat coming in through your windows by closing the drapes during the day, adding reflective window tint to southern windows, and hanging old-fashioned bamboo shades on the outside of heat-producing windows.

✔ **If you use an air conditioner to cool your house,
   turn the thermostat up a bit higher than the temperature you usually set.** If you normally set the
   A/C for 72 degrees Fahrenheit during the summer,
   switch to 78 degrees. When it's 95 degrees in the
   shade outside, 78 degrees still feels comfortable and
   not too warm. Also set the temperature higher for
   times when you're not there.

✔ **Use fans to circulate air.** Moving air feels several
   degrees cooler than still air. A ceiling fan can cool
   the whole room, but even a small box fan or oscillat-
   ing fan keeps the air moving.

✔ **Reduce how much heat you create inside your
   house:** Use your outdoor grill more often to keep
   from heating up the kitchen. Cook in the microwave,
   slow cooker, electric skillet, or toaster oven, rather
   than the stove and oven. Don't use the heat setting
   on your clothes dryer.

Warm Up for Less

• •

*S*tay cozy and still save money on your heating bills by following these hints.

Turn Down the Thermostat

The simplest way to save money on heating is to turn down your furnace a couple degrees. If you usually keep your thermostat set at 72 degrees Fahrenheit during the winter, turn it down to 70. If you're used to 70-degree temperatures, set the thermostat at 68. Lower the temperature even further at night when you're sleeping. Toss on an extra blanket if you're still a bit chilled.

Consider these other ways to stay warm without running up your heating bill:

- ✔ Close the vents and doors in rooms that aren't in use for long periods of time.

- ✔ A ceiling fan set to push air down keeps warm air circulating to the lower regions of the house.

- ✔ Higher humidity keeps the air warmer. Here are a couple of simple ideas to add warm moisture:

   • Let steamy air from the bathroom escape into the rest of the house after a shower.

- Boil water on the stovetop.

- Keep a kettle or pan full of water on top of your wood-burning stove or radiator.

Deal with Drafts

A well-insulated house can help you save quite a bit on your heating bills (and cooling bills, too). New houses are often built with energy-efficient features such as thermal-paned windows, well-insulated walls, and energy-efficient water heaters and furnaces. If you don't live in a newer house, consider using some of the following ideas to increase the benefits of your home's current heating system.

✔ Add a layer of air between your windows and the great outdoors (the air insulates much better than the window glass alone). Some ideas:

- If you have storm windows, use them.

- Stretch thick sheets of plastic across the inside of your window frames.

- Hang heavy curtains that you can pull closed at night. During the day, open your curtains, especially those on southern windows, for passive solar heating.

- After dark, hang blankets or quilts in front of the windows for added insulation. Install a decorative curtain rod above your existing window treatment, and then simply fold a blanket or quilt over the rod.

✔ Use a draft stopper at the bottom of outside doors. You can make one, buy an inexpensive one, or roll up a bathroom towel and place it next to the bottom of the door.

✔ Fill areas behind electric switch plates that are on outside walls with plastic foam or purchase plastic insulation that's already cut to size and made for this purpose.

✔ Close the flue on your fireplace when you're not using it. Leaving a fireplace flue open is like having a vacuum hose hooked to your house, sucking the warm air right out the chimney.

Make Your Own Cleaning Solutions

• •

*Y*ou don't need a cabinet full of the latest cleaners from your local supermarket. Rather, a few simple household ingredients can provide all you need to keep your house and appliances sparkling.

Three inexpensive and commonly available household products — white vinegar, baking soda, and bleach — can replace a variety of store-bought cleaners.

Many people also use ammonia as a cleaning staple. If you do as well, remember that ammonia combined with bleach or some other cleaning agents produces a toxic, or even deadly, gas. Never never *never* mix ammonia with any other cleaning product. For that matter, never mix any household cleaners, regardless of brand or type.

All cleaners, whether commercial or homemade, work best when left to sit for varying periods of time. Generally, the tougher the stain, the longer you let it sit to work.

White Vinegar

Full-strength white vinegar is an excellent cleaning option that kills many germs, bacteria, and molds. Keep a spray bottle of full-strength vinegar around the house, and spray it on countertops, toilet seats, doorknobs, and even cutting boards. Vinegar helps deodorize, and you can use it in your wash and get the same results as store-bought detergent additives.

Here are a few easy ideas for cleaning around the house with vinegar:

- Use full- or half-strength vinegar for cleaning windows, mirrors, chrome, and tile. (Wash your windows with newspapers to cut down on the lint left behind from cloth or paper towels.)

- To easily clean the microwave oven, heat ½ cup of white vinegar in a microwave-safe bowl or mug on high for 3 minutes. Let the vinegar sit undisturbed for about 15 minutes, and then remove the vinegar container and wipe down the inside of the microwave with a sponge and clear water.

- Use full-strength vinegar in the rinse-aid container of your dishwasher.

- Use about 1 cup of white vinegar and ¼ cup of baking soda (in addition to your laundry detergent) in place of store-bought bleaching products to whiten and brighten your clothes.

- Add ½ cup of white vinegar to the rinse cycle or pour it into the washing machine's fabric softener container to remove any leftover soap residue from the clothes. The clothes will smell clean and fresh.

Baking Soda

You can find bulk containers of baking soda in the baking supplies aisle of the supermarket. Baking soda is fairly inexpensive normally, but when you buy it in bulk, it's really a bargain. Baking soda works well for the following cleaning needs:

- Mix a 50/50 paste of baking soda and water for scrubbing bathtubs, tile, sinks, chrome, and pots and pans. Rinse thoroughly with water.

- Add about 1 teaspoon of baking soda to 1 cup of water, stir, and use in a spray bottle with a fine mist setting for an easy and inexpensive air freshener to spray around the room.

- Sprinkle a thin layer of baking soda in the bottom of the cat's litter box (before adding the kitty litter) to help cut the smell. Fluffy will thank you, and this can also prevent the need to buy more expensive deodorized kitty litter.

- Add about ¼ cup of baking soda to the washing machine's rinse cycle as a fabric softener and odor remover.

- Use a paste made from a mix of 50/50 baking soda and water to pretreat spots before putting the clothes in the wash.

Bleach

When it comes to killing germs and removing household mildew, you won't find a less expensive disinfectant and cleaning agent than common household bleach. Here are some simple cleaning ideas that use bleach:

✔ Use a 50/50 mixture of bleach and water to remove stubborn stains and mildew from tile and grout.

✔ Pour a 50/50 bleach-and-water mix into tea cups or coffee mugs with difficult stains. Allow them to soak overnight. The next day, pour out the bleach and water and wash the cup as usual.

✔ Mix 1 cup of bleach with 1 gallon of water for general cleaning and disinfecting, but be careful not to let the bleach mixture touch fabrics or anything that can have color bleached out of it (such as carpets, window treatments, clothing, and so on).

Spend less on lighting

After appliances and heating, indoor and outdoor lighting is one of the biggest electricity users in an average home. Cut down on the number of light bulbs turned on at any one time to save substantially on your electric bills. Here are some easy tips for lighting-related savings:

✔ If you have outdoor lighting for safety reasons, install motion detectors on the lights. They'll still come on when you need to see your way or if an intruder needs to be scared away.

✔ Replace frequently used light bulbs with fluorescent bulbs. They're a bit more expensive to buy, but they often last up to ten times longer than incandescent bulbs.

Replace a Roof Shingle

*B*ecause shingles become more flexible when warm, this task is best saved for a sunny day. Here's all you have to do:

1. **Fold back the shingle(s) above the one to be removed.**

2. **Use a flat pry bar to remove the nails that hold the damaged shingle in place.**

3. **Slip a new shingle in position to replace the one that was removed.**

4. **Nail the new shingle in place by using a flat pry bar as a hammer extension.**

   With this technique you can drive a nail in from beneath an overlapping shingle: First, press the nail into the shingle by hand. After the nail is in place, position the bottom of the flat bar so the straight end rests atop the nail head. As the hammer strikes the flat bar, the offset below drives the nail home.

#82

Find Roof Leaks

The first step in repairing a roof leak is finding its point of origin. Although finding a leak on a flat roof can be extremely difficult and should be left to an industry professional, do-it-yourselfers can find a leak on a pitched roof. To water test your roof, you need two people, one on the roof and one in the attic (or living space below if you don't have an attic). You also need the following tools:

- ✔ 1 ladder
- ✔ 1 garden hose
- ✔ 1 flashlight

Although water testing a pitched roof isn't a difficult process, it can be time-consuming and tedious, so be patient. Follow these steps:

1. **Station your partner in the attic and tell him or her to holler at the first sign of water.**

2. **Use the garden hose to run a modest amount of water over the roof at a point below the area where a leak is suspected.**

   Work from the lowest point of the roof (near the eaves or gutters) in an area about 4 to 6 feet wide. Work your way up the roof a couple of feet at a time. Stand on dry roofing above the water to help prevent a slip.

Don't run the hose full blast. Don't use a spray nozzle, and don't force the water between the shingles. Doing so may force water into the home, creating the illusion that you've found a leak when, in fact, you did nothing more than temporarily create one.

3. **The moment your helper sees water, he or she should let you know.**

   A wailing screech usually does the trick. Or use your cellphones to communicate without yelling.

After you find the leak, hire a contractor to repair it.

Add More Insulation

*M*ost home-maintenance projects save you money over time. But only a few of them produce an immediate and measurable return. Maintaining an energy-efficient home is one such project, and one of the best ways to do this is to make sure everything's properly insulated.

Attic Insulation

If you have loose fill insulation, look to see whether the insulation in your attic has shifted. If some areas of your ceiling are bare, solve the problem by using a plastic lawn rake to gently move the insulation from high spots onto the bald areas. (Be sure to use a plastic rake; with electrical wires present in the attic, it wouldn't be wise to use a metal rake.) You can also use a piece of batt insulation to cover a hole. Simply use a razor knife to cut batt insulation to the approximate length required and lay it in place.

If your insulation appears to be in good shape, but you still feel a chill, you may need to add more. Check with your local public utility or a local building inspector for advice on what to do.

Keep attic insulation clear of light fixtures. If the light boxes are covered with insulation, they can overheat, and a fire can result. And above all, don't plug attic vents. An attic must be able to breathe; otherwise, trapped hot air can convert even the best insulated home into a sweatbox on a hot summer day. In addition, a buildup of humidity can occur, which over time can result in wood rot, mildew, mold, and fungus growth.

Wall Insulation

Adding insulation to a wall is a bit more difficult than adding it to an attic. In an attic, the insulation is usually exposed. In a wall, the insulation resides between the interior and exterior wall coverings. To insulate a wall, you have to either remove the wall covering or create small penetrations and blow the insulation into the wall cavity. It's simply not cost-effective to remove a wall covering to insulate the wall cavity. Therefore, blown insulation is usually used to insulate the walls of a completed home.

Because wall studs are spaced every 16 inches or so, penetrations to add insulation must be made at the same intervals, thus filling one cavity at a time. In some homes, a horizontal block exists midway between the top and bottom of a wall cavity. In such cases, two penetrations must be made into each cavity: one above the horizontal block and one below it.

Floor Insulation

An insulated floor substantially reduces the loss of heat, helps to eliminate mildew- and rot-causing condensation, and generally helps to keep your toes warm when you go barefoot through the kitchen.

Periodically crawl beneath your home with a flashlight to check the condition of the floor insulation in your basement or sub-area. You want to ensure that it's properly positioned. Sagging is the biggest problem. Floor insulation is normally held in place (between the floor joist) with netting or bailing wire attached from one joist-bottom to another. If the insulation netting sags, reattach or replace it.

Lightning rods (named for their speedy installation) are a handy alternative to netting or bailing wire when maintaining sagging floor insulation. These lightweight, flexible steel rods hold the insulation in place by spring tension. You place one end of the rod against the side of a floor joist and bend it slightly so the other end is forced into place against the face of the opposite joist. Use one hand to hold the insulation up and the other hand to whip the lightning rod into place.

Insulate Pipes

* *

*P*utting insulation around all accessible water pipes saves energy, prevents freezing during most moderate to medium chills, and reduces condensation when pipes flow through attics and crawlspaces.

Properly maintained pipe insulation can be cheap insurance. A pipe that bursts in the attic can destroy a substantial portion of your home before the leak is stopped.

Be sure the tape that holds the insulation in place is in good shape, and make sure the insulation is still in good condition, as well. If either the insulation or the tape crumbles to the touch, the material should be replaced.

Pre-formed, tubular, foam pipe insulation is slit lengthwise for easy installation. All you have to do is open the slit and lay the insulation onto the pipe. Pipe insulation comes in 6-foot lengths and is easy to cut with scissors or a razor knife.

Insulate Heat Ducts

As with other kinds of insulation, the material that surrounds your heat ducts reduces energy costs while improving the effectiveness of your central heating and cooling system. It also helps prevent unwanted condensation in attics and crawlspaces, thereby reducing the chance for mold, mildew, and the foul odors associated with them.

Wrap insulation around and around the duct in a corkscrew fashion. Air currents, rodents, house movement, and vibration in the heating system can cause the insulation to loosen and fall away from the ducting. While you're there, add an extra layer if your budget allows. It can't hurt.

 You can hold insulation together by "stitching" a nail into it. Simply insert the nail the same way a seamstress uses a sewing pin to hold two pieces of fabric together.

Test and Fix a Window Air Leak

*A*ir leaks mean excessive energy loss — and cost. Summer or winter, you don't want your house to leak air, especially when you spend your hard-earned dollars warming or cooling it.

Test a window for leaks by holding a lighted candle near all its joints and connections. If the candle flickers, you have an air leak. Check

- Where one section of the window meets another
- Where the windows meet the frame
- Where the frame meets the wall

To fix air leaks, try these tactics:

- **Caulk around the window:** Often air leaks at a window result from a breakdown in the connection between the frame of the window and the frame of the house. To prevent leaks, caulk the window where its frame meets the exterior siding. If the window is surrounded by wood trim, seal all gaps between the trim and the siding (and the trim and the window frame) with a high-grade polyurethane caulk.

✔ **Replace the weatherstripping:** Leaks occur when weatherstripping wears out. You may have to remove the operable portion of the window to find the weatherstripping. Most home centers sell replacement weatherstripping in peel-and-stick rolls. If you aren't sure about what to do, take the section you removed to the store with you, or snap a picture of the area that needs attention and take it with you. A picture is definitely worth a thousand words!

✔ **Inject foam sealant between the frame of the window and the frame of the house.** This is a major deterrent to air infiltration and also prevents water from leaking into the house.

Stop Air Leaks around Doors

An air leak in a door frame is pretty common. As the moisture content changes in soil, your home shifts. Your doors also shift, creating gaps large enough for a dump truck to pass through.

You can add foam sealant between the frame of the door and the frame of the house by removing the interior door casing. The casing is the wood trim that covers the joint between the door frame and the wall. Use a flat pry bar to slowly remove the trim so you don't damage it.

Other air leaks can occur between the door and the door frame. This is where weatherstripping is handy. It doesn't make any difference whether the exterior door is painted or stained, large or small, solid wood or French style, the same type of weatherstripping can be used.

An easy-to-find and -install weatherstripping consists of a rubber bead attached lengthwise to a strip of metal. Standing outside the door, with the door in the closed position, gently press the rubber portion of the weatherstripping against the door and frame at the same time. Attach the metal section of the weatherstripping to the door frame with the nails or screws provided. Here, oblong holes allow the weatherstripping to be adjusted later as house movement causes the door to shift.

Identify Plumbing Leaks

*W*ater leaks can be expensive, not only for the damage they cause (think rot and mildew), but also because you're stuck paying for the leaking water, even if, as is the case with some leaks, you don't know you have one.

If you're on a public water system, you have a water meter somewhere on or near your property. Besides telling you how much water you're using, it can also help you detect leaks.

Take a meter reading, and then turn off every plumbing fixture in your house (including the built-in icemaker or other water-consuming appliances) for a couple of hours. After everything is off, take another meter reading. If the reading changes, you have a leak. You can tell how much water you've used in any given timeframe by subtracting the first reading from the second reading. A cubic foot contains 7½ gallons of water.

If you find a leak, you need to identify where it's coming from and fix it or call a professional to help out.

Improve Water Heater Efficiency

• •

*1*f your water heater is located in a garage or basement, or you don't want the heat the water heater emits into the area, install a heavy insulation blanket — R-11 or better. Doing so improves the water heater's energy efficiency and reduces the ambient heat. The R value relates to the thickness of the blanket; the higher the R value, the thicker the blanket, and the more insulating horsepower.

You can purchase a water heater insulation blanket as a kit based on the size of the heater — 30, 40, 50 gallons, and so on. The kit contains a blanket that has white vinyl on the outside and raw insulation on the inside and enough adhesive tape to finish the seams.

If you have a gas water heater, wrap the blanket all the way around and from the top to just below the controller. Don't worry if the blanket seems a bit short. Remember, the bottom of the tank is several inches above the very bottom of the water heater.

Don't wrap the top, because the insulation could catch fire from the heat being exhausted. Also, the blanket shouldn't cover the controller, the anode, or the pressure and temperature relief valve.

If you have an electric water heater, wrap the sides and the top (an electric water heater doesn't have an exhaust). But don't cover the access panels for elements; otherwise, these could overheat.

You don't need a blanket if your water heater is located where its lost heat can be felt and appreciated. Nor do you need one if you have a new water heater that's factory insulated with R-16 or better. The manufacturer's label will tell you how much insulation your water heater contains (the factory-installed insulation is located between the metal shell and the tank, so don't freak if you can't see it).

Help Your Furnace Work More Efficiently

*T*he best way to ensure that your heating system is as energy efficient as it can be is to do routine maintenance. (If you have an electric system, it requires virtually no maintenance. In fact, you have to do only two things: Vacuum the convectors once a month [if you have them] and pay the electricity bill.)

Routine annual inspection and cleaning by a qualified, licensed contractor can keep your system running for many years without trouble. Don't be pennywise and pound-foolish. A dirty, inefficient furnace costs you ten times that much in wasted fuel. Beyond that, you can do the following:

✔ **For forced-air systems:** Replace the furnace filter regularly (every month during the heating season, and every month year round if an air-conditioning system is part of the same system) and check the ducts, which distribute warmed air to various locations throughout the house, for leaks. If you see fuzz or feel warm air coming out through the joints between duct segments, seal them with metal tape.

Although filters cost only a couple of bucks apiece, don't buy filters one at a time — get a whole case. They're cheaper by the dozen.

✔ **For hot-water systems:** Most hot-water systems have only a single gauge, which measures three things: pressure, temperature, and altitude (the height of the water in the system). It's important to monitor the pressure. Most boilers run with only 12 to 15 pounds of pressure. The boiler can become seriously damaged and even dangerous if the pressure exceeds 30 pounds. If the pressure is abnormally high, you may have a waterlogged expansion tank that can be drained. You can drain the expansion tank yourself (use the owner's manual for information or a home-maintenance book for guidance) or call a repairperson.

You also may need to bleed the air out of the radiator. To do so, just turn the bleed valve about a quarter-turn counterclockwise and keep the screwdriver or radiator key in the valve. If you hear a hissing sound, that's good — it's air escaping. As soon as the hissing stops and you see a dribble of water come out, close the valve.

Don't open the valve more than is necessary; hot water will come rushing out before you can close it. At the very least, you'll make a wet mess. At the very worst, you could be scalded.

✔ **For steam systems:** Most adjustments to your steam boiler should be performed by a pro. But you can do three important things yourself:

   • **Check the steam gauge on a regular basis.** Make sure it's within the normal range. If it isn't, shut the system down immediately and call for service.

- **Check the safety valve every month.** Located on the top of the boiler, this valve vents excess pressure if the boiler goes crazy and exceeds safe levels. When the system is hot, push down on the handle to see whether steam comes out. Make sure to stand away from the outlet — the steam is boiling hot. If no steam comes out, call a serviceman to replace the valve immediately.

- **Check the water level once a month.** The water-level gauge has valves on each side. Open them both and make sure the water level is in the middle, and then close the valves. If you don't see any water, shut off the boiler, let it cool down, and add water.

Save on Your Fuel Expenses

• •

*R*educing your speed is one way to save on fuel. Getting a car with better gas mileage is another. While anyone can do the former, you're probably not going to seriously consider doing the latter unless you're in the market for a new car anyway. Regardless of the car you have, you can do several things to maximize your fuel efficiency.

Look under the Hood

You may be surprised at all the "little" things that can negatively affect your gas mileage:

- ✔ A dirty air filter can cause you to lose 1 mile per gallon at 50 miles per hour.

- ✔ A poorly functioning PCV valve, which recycles the exhaust fumes back into the intake manifold to be re-burned, makes your engine run less efficiently.

- ✔ Spark plugs that misfire can cost you up to 25 percent in gas mileage.

- ✔ Accessory belts (those that connect your fan, water pump, alternator, and a variety of other devices) that are too loose or too tight can result in a serious loss of efficiency.

> ✔ A poorly adjusted brake may "drag" while the vehicle is in motion. The result is that your brake linings — and the gas in your tank — won't last as long.

Take a look at these parts of your vehicle and make sure that they're in good condition and are functioning properly. A simple tuneup can reduce carbon monoxide and hydrocarbon exhaust emissions by 30 to 50 percent, save you fuel, and improve your vehicle's performance. If you can cut your fuel consumption by only 10 percent, you save an average of 77 gallons a year!

Fill 'Er Up

What you do at the pump affects your fuel consumption and can save you money as well.

In hot weather, fill up in the early morning or evening, when the air is cooler. Like everything else, gasoline expands with heat. An increase of 30 degrees can cause 10 gallons of gas to expand by as much as four-fifths of a quart — that's as much as a bottle of whiskey!

Change Your Own Car Oil

*C*hanging oil is easy. In fact, unless your oil filter and/or oil drain plug is impossible to reach, you have good reasons to change your oil and oil filter yourself. It's cheaper, you know that the job's being done right, and it requires little time or effort.

You'll need these supplies: oil and an oil filter (make sure it's the right one for your car), an adjustable wrench (to unscrew the oil drain plug), a container to catch the oil (make sure it's low enough to fit under your car), a funnel, and some rags.

Follow these easy steps:

1. **Warm up your engine for 2 or 3 minutes so the gook gets churned up and can flow out of the engine easily.**

   You don't want the engine so hot that you burn yourself. When it's slightly warm, shut off the engine.

2. **Look under your car to find the drain plug.**

   The drain plug is a large nut or plug located under the oil pan at the bottom of the engine. If you can't reach your oil drain plug easily, you'll have to either crawl under your car to reach it or jack up the car.

3. **Push the container under the oil drain plug so it can catch the oil.**

4. **Protecting your hand with a rag or some paper towels, unscrew the oil drain plug (be ready to move your hand out of the way).**

   The oil now drains out of your engine into the container. While the oil drains, get out from under the car and take a look under the hood.

5. **Remove the cap from the oil filler hole at the top of your engine and unscrew the oil filter, using a wrench if you can't do it by hand.**

   The oil filter looks like a tin can screwed to the side of your engine. To unscrew it, twist it counterclockwise. The filter will have oil in it, so be careful not to spill it when you remove it. If any remnants of the filter's rubber seal remain on your engine, remove them.

   On some vehicles, you can easily reach the oil filter by leaning under the hood. Other car manufacturers place the filter so it must be reached from under the car. If this describes your vehicle, you'll have to get under it.

6. **Empty the oil from the filter into the drain pan.**

   After the filter is empty, wrap it in newspaper and set it aside to take to a recycling center with your old oil.

7. **While the old oil drains out of the engine, open a new bottle of oil.**

8. **Dip a finger in the new oil and moisten the gasket on the top of the new oil filter. Then screw the new filter into the engine where the old one was.**

   Follow directions on the filter, or turn it gently until it "seats" and then give it another three-quarter turn.

   Unless the filter manufacturer recommends it, or your hand can't fit in the space, don't use an oil filter wrench to tighten the filter. It should fit tightly, but you don't want to crush the gasket, or the filter will leak.

9. **Reach under the car again and use your dirty rag to wipe around the place where the oil drain plug goes.**

10. **Replace the oil drain plug and use an adjustable wrench to tighten it.**

    If your vehicle uses an oil drain plug gasket, make sure the old one has been removed and lay a new gasket on the pan before you replace the plug.

11. **After you install the oil filter and replace the oil drain plug, use a funnel to pour all but 1 quart of the fresh oil into the oil filler hole.**

12. **Replace the oil filler cap and run the engine for 30 to 60 seconds while you check for leaks from the oil drain plug and around the filter.**

    The oil pressure light on your dashboard should go out in 10 or 15 seconds (or if your car has an oil pressure gauge, the needle should move off "Low"). Your oil pressure is low to zero while the light is on, until your oil filter fills up. If the light doesn't go out, check under the car and around the engine for leaks. Running the engine circulates oil into the new filter, and because filters hold a half to a full quart of oil, you want to be sure that your filter is full to get an accurate reading on the oil dipstick.

13. **Shut off the engine and wait 5 to 10 minutes for the oil to settle into the oil pan and then check the oil level again.**

    Remove the oil dipstick, wipe it with a clean, lint-free rag, and shove it back in. Pull it out again and check it. Keep adding oil a little at a time and checking the stick until you reach the "Full" line on the dipstick.

14. **Remove the drain pan from under the vehicle and give the car a test drive.**

    Go around the block a couple of times; then let the oil settle down again and recheck the dipstick and the dashboard indicator.

15. **Fill out the Maintenance Record at the back of your Owner's Manual (or wherever you keep track of your regular auto maintenance).**

Dispose of the old oil by taking it to an auto parts store or other oil recycling center.

Take Care of Your Tires

T ires don't require a great deal of maintenance, but the jobs in this section will pay off handsomely by increasing your tires' longevity, handling, and performance, as well as providing you with a more comfortable ride and better gas mileage.

Check Tire Pressure

The single most important factor in caring for your tires is maintaining the correct inflation pressure. You should check your tires once a month and before every long trip to see that they're properly inflated. Underinflated tires wear out faster, create excessive heat, increase fuel consumption, and make the vehicle harder to handle. Overinflated tires can blow out more easily, wear out faster, and make the vehicle unstable and unsafe to handle.

To check the air pressure, you need to buy a tire pressure gauge at a hardware store or auto supply store (they're not expensive) and determine the proper air pressure for your tires. Look for the proper inflation pressure on the tire decal. You can find the tire decal on one of the doors, door pillars, glove box, console, or trunk.

Then follow these steps:

1. **Remove the little cap from the tire valve that sticks out of your tire near the wheel rim.**

2. **Place the open, rounded end of the tire gauge against the valve so that the little pin in the gauge contacts the pin in the valve.**

3. **Press the gauge against the valve stem.**

   You'll hear a hissing sound as air starts to escape from the tire. You'll also see a little stick emerge from the other end of the tire gauge. It emerges partway almost as soon as the air starts to hiss and stops emerging almost immediately.

4. **Without pushing the stick back in, remove the gauge from the tire valve.**

5. **Without touching the stick, look at the numbers on it. Pay attention to the last number showing.**

   This number is the amount of air pressure in your tire.

6. **Add air if necessary.**

   If the number on the gauge is lower than the recommended pressure, you need to add air. Follow the steps in "Add Air to Your Tires."

7. **Repeat these steps for each tire, including the spare.**

Add Air to Your Tires

If your tires appear to be low, note the amount that they're underinflated, drive to a local gas station, and follow these steps:

1. **Park your vehicle so you can reach all four tires with the air hose.**

2. **Remove the cap from the tire valve on the first tire.**

3. **Use your tire gauge to check the air pressure in the tire and see how much it's changed so you can add the same amount of air that the tire lacked before you drove it to the station.**

   The pressure will have increased because driving causes the tires to heat up and the air inside them to expand.

4. **Use the air hose to add air in short bursts, checking the pressure each time with your tire gauge and making adjustments as necessary.**

   If you add too much air, let some out by pressing the pin on the tire valve with the back of the air hose nozzle or with the little knob on the back of the rounded end of the tire gauge.

Hire a Pro without Getting Taken for a Ride

● ●

*S*everal kinds of shops repair and service vehicles: dealerships, chain stores, specialists, and independents. Dealerships usually stock a wide variety of original parts and equipment made specifically for your vehicle, but they're often more expensive than other types of service facilities. Save money by choosing another option. But how do you decide which is the right shop for you? Each has its drawbacks as well as its advantages.

- ✔ **Chain and department stores:** These are generally less expensive than dealerships. They usually stock a wide variety of parts, and provide guarantees on parts and labor. Many also accept coupon and discount mailers from competitors. The downside is that the technicians may get a commission on the parts they sell, motivating them to sell you a new part instead of repairing an old one.

- ✔ **Independents:** Many independent shops are less expensive than dealerships. The best independents offer honest, reliable, and experienced independent mechanics who provide personalized service based on high standards of excellence. An unreliable one patches things together, uses cheap parts, and hopes for the best.

✔ **Specialists:** There are two types of specialists: A specialized chain store or independent mechanic who deals with a specific type of repair, such as brakes, transmissions, or mufflers, or an independent shop that works only on specific makes or types of vehicles, such as imports, motorcycles, or vans. Check out national chains in consumer publications such as *Consumer Reports* to be sure that the one you choose has a good reputation for durable parts and quality service.

Several organizations test, rate, and certify good service facilities or individual technicians. If you're unsure about a particular shop, look for a sign or a patch on a technician's uniform showing that the shop or the individual has achieved recognition from one of the following sources:

✔ **AAA- and CAA-approved repair facilities:** Approved by both the American Automobile Association (AAA) and the Canadian Automobile Association (CAA).

✔ **ASE-certified technicians:** The National Institute for Automotive Service Excellence (ASE) certifies technicians by testing them on a variety of automobile repair specialties.

✔ **IGO (Independent Garage Owners Association):** An IGO shield or sign indicates that the owner of the garage is a member of the IGO, which, although it doesn't qualify individual technicians, has a code of ethics that members pledge to live up to if they want to stay in the organization.

✔ **Better Business Bureau:** Check with your local Better Business Bureau to see whether a shop has been the subject of numerous consumer complaints.

✔ **Referrals:** Probably the best way to find a good mechanic is the same way you find a doctor, lawyer, or plumber — through referrals. Ask people who drive the same make vehicle as you do where they go for repairs, and then check out the shops. As a fringe benefit of these conversations, you'll also know which shops to avoid.

Part V

Making the Most of Holidays and Other Special Events

The 5th Wave   By Rich Tennant

"Of course I'm proud to be married to a policeman. I just don't want to decorate every holiday with orange traffic cones and crime scene tape."

In this part . . .

*H*olidays and special events are times to celebrate and enjoy. They're also times when your budget and bank account can take a real hit. Fortunately, you don't have to do without; you just have to do a little differently. The key is to figure out what's most important and to put your resources and energy there. If you figure out what's nonnegotiable — spending quality time with your family or giving from the heart rather than the wallet, for example — you may just discover that although you spend less, you give more.

Throw a Party on a Budget

● ●

*P*lanning a party can be just as fun as attending one. And when your planning lets you save money at the same time, well, that's icing on the cake. The simplest and most important trick is to plan ahead and put together a party budget.

When you budget for your party, do so *before* you start shopping. List the items you need and estimate what you can afford to spend on each item. Keep a running total of the expenses so you know when you need to cut corners on one item because you went over on another.

Check out the following budget-saving ideas:

- **Always shop from a detailed list.** Impulse buys are common in party planning. Those corn-shaped corncob holders would be a hit at the barbecue, but are they necessary?

- **Use reuseable tableware.** Using real dishes, utensils, and glassware can save big money.

- **Prepare the food yourself.** Bake your own cake or serve sliced homemade snack cakes instead of ordering a personalized cake from the grocery store.

- **Make and deliver your own invitations.** Save on postage by hand-delivering invitations to people you see regularly. E-mail invitations are acceptable for casual parties.

✔ **Aim for a simple, balanced menu.** For a dinner party, a simple snack or appetizer, salad or soup, vegetables, and a main course followed by a simple dessert make a nice, well-rounded meal.

The key to entertaining on a budget without sacrificing flair is to think *presentation*. You can make anything look special: a tray of cold cuts on a bed of curly lettuce, utensils standing in a cup tied in ribbon, napkins folded into birds. And for those extra special occasions when you want to splurge a little without breaking the bank? A standing rib roast is a wower, but so is a crown roast — and it's less than half the cost.

Entertain on a Shoestring

Do you want to socialize with friends and family while spending as little money as possible? Keep in mind that the real focus of the party is the guests — good food is just an added bonus! Here are a few ideas that are proven winners.

Covered-Dish Dinners

Hosts provide the main course, and guests bring side dishes and desserts. The benefits of this type of gathering are that no one has too much work or cost to absorb and everyone gets to try lots of new and varied dishes. Bring the kids and hire one babysitter or older child to sit or entertain the children in the basement (or in a separate part of the house), and the adults can visit or play cards upstairs or in the living room.

Wine-Tasting Party

This type of get-together can be an educational and fun experience (and not to mention thrifty). Here's how it works: The host's responsibilities are to invite friends or family, lay out the rules, and provide glasses, crackers, fruit, and cheese for all. Then guests each bring a bottle of wine. The host predetermines the rules, such as the following: Bring red wine, $10 per bottle maximum, with bottles disguised in paper bags. After all the guests have arrived, randomly number the bags, open the wine bottles, and begin the tasting. Discuss the characteristics and qualities of each wine and vote on your favorite while enjoying your cheese, fruit, and crackers and the company of your friends. At the end, unveil the winning selection.

Game Night

Invite two to four people over after dinner to play Farkel (a dice game of skill and luck; all you need are six dice and the instructions, which you can find online) or another game of your choice.

Spend Less on Holiday Decorations and Gifts

● ●

*Y*ou can have festive holiday celebrations without dipping into savings or running up a credit card balance. Use these ideas to jump-start your creativity and see where your imagination takes you!

Easter

Ahh, Easter: warm spring weather, newborn bunnies, and freshly cut tulips. If only those store-bought springtime goodies, like Easter baskets for the kids and decorations for the home, weren't so expensive. But with a little creativity, you can enjoy the season frugally.

For instance, you can make your own inexpensive Easter baskets. Use wicker baskets, which last year after year, or be creative with your choice of container. Paper bags, Easter bonnets, and colorful plastic sand pails are all great options. Fill your bags or baskets with treats that you accumulate throughout the year — crayons, bubbles, chopsticks, stickers, and little cookies and candies.

Halloween

Halloween costumes don't have to scare the living daylights out of your budget. Even a simple homemade gypsy or hobo costume can be loads of frightening fun, especially if the children design it themselves. Make the following inexpensive costumes from things found around the house or at thrift stores:

- **Ghost:** Use a permanent marker to draw some details on a sheet, like spider webs or fake bloodstains. If you add an old chain or two and tie a large white handkerchief around the top of the child's head and under his jaw, you've created Jacob Marley from Dickens's *A Christmas Carol*.

- **Tacky Tourist:** Just put together a Hawaiian shirt, sunglasses, a hat, a camera, white sunblock on the nose (just use white face paint), a large bag or purse, and maps or tourist brochures peeking out of a few pockets.

- **Ladybug:** Dress your child in a pair of black leggings and a plain long-sleeved black shirt. Remove the arms from a large red sweatshirt (bought at a thrift store) and pin, glue, or draw large black dots all over and a stripe down the middle of the sweatshirt. Fashion antennae with black pipe cleaners.

Shop off-season to get the best deals. Halloween decorations are cheaper right after Halloween; limit yourself to one or two new items at the end of the season and store them with your current decorations.

Hanukkah and Christmas

Holiday giving and frugal living don't have to be polar opposites if you follow these easy ideas:

- ✓ **Create homemade wrapping paper.** Make your own wrapping paper out of brown paper grocery bags, inexpensive kitchen sponges (the softer, the better), and craft paint. Cut open the paper bags and spread them flat, with the plain insides of the bags facing up. Cut the sponges into simple holiday shapes (snow-men, trees, stars), dip them into red, green, or white paint, and then sponge-paint randomly over the open paper bags. Tied with inexpensive brown twine, this makes a rustic and beautiful gift-wrapping idea — plus it's a fun holiday family activity, too.

  Newspaper comics also make bright, fun wrapping paper.

- ✓ **Find post-holiday deals.** If you like the variety and sparkle of store-bought paper, shop for it after the holidays, when it's half off or more.

- ✓ **Limit the number of decorations.** A few strategically placed decorations can have a dramatic effect. A seasonal decoration on the front door, a tree in the living room, a centerpiece on the dining table, and a few fragrant candles around the house can set the mood just as well as animated Santas dancing in every window.

- ✓ **Save on gifts.** Set a limit on how much to spend on each person you're buying for. Shop early. Shop online. Purchase gifts on clearance throughout the year. If you buy gifts for extended family members, agree to a spending limit, buy a single family gift rather than individual gifts, or trade names.

Get Creative with Gift Giving

• •

*G*iving to others is definitely wonderful, but is going to the store and paying top dollar for household clutter really the answer? Probably not. Here are some gift ideas to help you think creatively:

✔ **A personalized calendar:** Creating a personalized calendar can be as simple as buying a store-bought calendar and writing important family days to remember throughout the year, such as birthdays, anniversaries, and so on. Or buy a blank calendar at the rubber stamp store and decorate the entire calendar yourself. Add the important family dates to the calendar, and then when the year's over, the recipient can cut off the calendar section and keep the scrapbook pages together as a memory book. Instead of photos or artwork at the top of each calendar page, how about using a simple layout design with favorite family recipes, quotations, and so forth?

✔ **Favorite family recipes:** Many families pass down favorite recipes almost like treasured family heirlooms. Request that family members send you a couple of their favorite recipes and maybe even a sentence or two about each recipe, its history or origin, any traditions surrounding the recipe, or even funny family stories. Then put together your own cookbook or have the booklets professionally copied and bound (which is still relatively inexpensive).

✔ **Coffee mug or tea cup with a tasty treat:** Include a selection of small bags of coffee mix or favorite coffee beans, spiced cider mix, a selection of gourmet teas, a pretty silver-plated spoon found at a thrift store, or other favorite tea time or coffee break treats. Wrap it all in cellophane and tie with a pretty ribbon.

✔ **A box of loving memories:** Save small souvenirs (theater tickets, seashells, matchbooks with restaurant logos, and so on) from previous dates or activities you shared with your loved one. Put them into a special gift box on an anniversary or a "just because" day. For the friend or relative far from home, this can make an especially meaningful gift.

✔ **Cotton scraps for your favorite seamstress:** Small pieces of colorful fabric can be used in a variety of creative ways, so if you have a sewing or quilting fanatic in your circle of friends, keep your eyes open while you're at garage sales for cotton shirts, sheets, and pillowcases in nice patterns or plain colors. Pick scraps in colors that blend well together. Cut out large squares of useable material from the backs and fronts of the shirts, fold the material into neat squares, and then tie a ribbon around the stack of colorful scraps.

✔ **A dress-up bin:** Stock up on inexpensive dress-up clothes and accessories: prom dresses, hats, shawls, scarves, cowboy paraphernalia, costumes, surgical attire, costume jewelry, men's suit jackets, clip-on ties, and fancy shoes. (Go through your own closets or get them at garage sales and thrift stores.) Old lace tablecloths and curtains make perfect wedding veils. Plastic bins with lids work well for storage, but even just a big cardboard box covered with wrapping paper can work for this much-appreciated gift.

✔ **A gift basket for the whole family:** A large popcorn bowl full of microwave popcorn packages, candy, and movie rental gift cards is a great idea.

✔ **Time, donations, and services:** Instead of buying more items to clutter up family's and friends' homes, many people give alternative gifts that are more in keeping with their personal priorities and the spirit of each season. Some alternative gift ideas include making a donation of time, energy, and resources to a charity in your friend's name and putting together a homemade coupon book of personalized jobs you'll do for the recipient: Mow the lawn, give a back rub, take him shopping, and so on.

Great gift-basket ideas

Gift basket are one-of-a-kind presents that speak louder than words. Be serious. Be silly. Be inventive. But above all, have fun. Here are gift basket themes to get your creative juices flowing:

✔ Guys' Night: Almonds and a DVD of football's greatest bloopers

✔ Midnight Icebox Raid: Snacks stashed in an old cookie jar from a flea market or garage sale

✔ Sunday Brunch: Traditional brunch foods, Bloody Mary mix, and the Sunday paper

✔ Gay Paree: Pâté, a French-translation dictionary, and an Edith Piaff CD

✔ Right-O: Scones, a teapot, a selection of teas, and a book of Keats's odes

✔ Home on the Range: Barbecue sauce, a flameproof barbecue mitt, and a set of steak knives

✔ Girls' Night Out: Chocolate truffles, a video of Love Story, and a box of tissues

Give and Package Sweets and Treats

Homemade gifts send the message that you care enough to take the time to make something with your own two hands. Anyone would enjoy homemade gifts from the kitchen any time of year — whether you have a reason for giving or not. Give them to celebrate holidays, to mark birthdays and anniversaries, to spread cheer to someone who's not well, or for no reason at all.

Put just as much care into the way you package your gift as you do into making it in the first place. Keep a few containers, bags, or wraps on hand. They're convenient for spontaneous gift giving, so try to get in the habit of looking for these things when you're shopping. Consider the following a guided tour of places to look. You never know what unusual packaging you may be the first to discover.

✔ **Craft stores:** Roam the aisles and you're sure to discover all sorts of boxes, ribbon, baskets, papers, pipe cleaners, crepe paper, twine, raffia, twisties, and doodads.

✔ **Super discount stores:** Check out the toy department and see what's available in the way of buckets and such. The card departments carry cute little shopping bags. Housewares departments have napkins, mugs, and canisters.

✓ **Gourmet food shops:** These shops probably have the traditional food containers, including the fancier decorative bottles and French canning jars. These items are great if they fit within your budget.

✓ **Party goods stores:** Seasonal ideas are usually available in party goods stores. Wrapping paper, ribbon, tissue paper, and colorful napkins are standard items.

✓ **Flea markets and related places:** Flea markets, antique stores, garage sales, and tag sales are great sources for potential containers and wrapping items. Beautiful old glass, baskets, advertising containers, linens, bowls, teacups, wine glasses, molds, and crockery are all there for the creating.

✓ **Your own house:** Home is where the heart is, and it's also the starting point for finding recyclables. Reuse unusual glass water bottles (some water companies use colored bottles) by adding a cork and sealing it with paraffin. Reuse pretty tins left over from commercial cookies. Cut up old greeting cards and use them for tags or appliqués.

✓ **Fabric and notions stores:** Go here if you want to wrap your gift in cloth, whether it's topping a jam jar with a square of gingham or wrapping the whole present in a fabric bundle through the Japanese art of *furoshiki*.

✓ **Stationery and card stores:** They always have the usual wrapping paper, tissue, and cards, but more and more stores are expanding their lines to carry little tote bags and tins.

✓ **Garden centers and florists:** Garden shops carry all sorts of containers in varying shapes nowadays, including pots and baskets. Many garden stores also carry patio tableware in all shapes, colors, and sizes.

✔ **Hardware stores:** Look in the paint department for disposable cardboard paint buckets. Empty reusable metal paint buckets are another option. In the plumbing department, buy a short section of PVC pipe to fill with individually wrapped candies or cookies and then wrap it in stiff fabric or paper like a gigantic party popper.

Everything food comes in contact with should be food safe. If you're not sure, wrap the gift in food wrap first.

Fun food-as-gift facts

Here are a few random thoughts to keep in mind about giving food as gifts:

✔ Keep the recipient's tastes and preferences in mind, especially if you're including a reusable container. For example, even if you don't really like contemporary decor, if the recipient does, choose a container appropriate for her tastes, not yours.

✔ The container in which you give the gift isn't always the best container in which to store the food. Don't forget to mention this fact to the recipient.

✔ Date and label food gifts. Tell the recipient how long a gift will last. If you suspect that anyone has a food allergy or if you want to be on the safe side, give a list of ingredients. At the very least, identify whether the gift contains nuts.

✔ Keep perishable gifts refrigerated until the last minute before giving. Make sure the recipient knows the gift is perishable.

#100

Save on Fine Dining

Dinner out in a nice restaurant doesn't have to become a vaguely remembered activity. By following some simple suggestions, families and couples can enjoy an occasional dinner out for a small price tag.

✔ **Avoid overpriced drinks.** A simple cup of coffee can cost at least $2, and sodas, milk, and juice for the kids are usually more than that. Drinking water can often cut $10 or more from the cost of a typical family's meal. To make the water special, ask for a lemon or lime wedge.

If the nicer drinks are essential to your dining experience, forego the mixed drinks; they're usually more expensive than a glass of wine or a beer. Also, many nicer restaurants allow you to bring wine. They generally charge an uncorking fee, but that's significantly less expensive than buying your wine from them.

✔ **Fill up on appetizers or share a meal.** Appetizers are generally less expensive, just as yummy, and nice to linger over, and you can buy two or more for the price you'd spend on a meal. And given portion sizes today, one meal can often easily feed two people, so share. Even if you have to pay a small fee, it's still less expensive.

✔ **Be aware of suggestive sales.** Keep in mind when ordering in a restaurant that anything extra or suggested by the waiter is going to add to your bill. If you really want ice cream on your slice of pie, fine. But if you're only saying yes because what the waitress suggested suddenly sounds delicious, you've succumbed to suggestive sales. Keep your radar alert when someone starts suggesting additional things to eat or drink.

✔ **Choose your dining time wisely.** Many restaurants have reduced-rate menus on certain days or during particular hours.

✔ **Keep your eye out for advertisements and coupons.** You can often find these in the weekly advertising circulars that come in the mail and the newspaper. Many places offer half-price appetizers. Or you may find an ad for buy-one-get-one-free dinner specials. Some restaurants even advertise free meals for kids during certain hours or on particular days of the week. Also, always ask for the restaurant's special of the day. It's often $2 to $5 cheaper than the rest of the main menu items.

Part VI

Staying Afloat If the Boat Starts to Sink

The 5th Wave   By Rich Tennant

Tell Her Highness I think the people from the collection agency are here.

In this part . . .

In a time when prices keep going up and incomes seem to keep going down, making ends meet can be more challenging than ever. Let a crisis happen — a major medical problem or a job loss, for example — and the situation just gets worse. If you're feeling overwhelmed with debt or are facing the real possibility of losing your home or having to declare bankruptcy, this part is for you. It doesn't offer any quick fixes, but it does give advice on how to put your credit back in good standing and navigate your way through major financial catastrophes.

Look for Signs of Financial Trouble

Although money problems often seem to strike without warning, they usually give off some indicators that you're headed for trouble. You and your partner (if you have one) should remain on the lookout for warning signs and work together to build a strong financial foundation that can protect you from foreclosure. Here are some red flags:

- ✔ **An unbalanced budget:** You should have at least as much money coming in as is flowing out each month. If you have a partner, the two of you should agree, upfront, on how much to spend and what to spend it on.

- ✔ **Unpaid bills:** If you've missed more than one mortgage payment, you're most likely confronting serious financial difficulties — and you're closer to major calamity than you may realize.

  When bills arrive, prioritize them and pay them as soon as possible so they don't stack up.

✔ **Unregulated spending:** If you end up surprised by how quickly your money disappears or frequently think you have a bill covered only to discover that the money is gone, chances are you're not keeping track of what you're spending money on. The situation can be exacerbated if you have a partner. If you're both off spending money on your own pet luxuries, problems often arise.

✔ **Spending too much on debt:** If more than 20 percent of your monthly take-home income goes toward paying off debt, not including your mortgage or rent, you may be ready for some professional help.

✔ **Inability to make minimum payments:** If you can barely afford to make minimum payments, chances are you can't afford to save — and that puts you at risk for ending up deeper in debt from unexpected illness, car problems, or temporary unemployment.

✔ **Arguing with your partner about finances:** Fighting about money is going to happen at one time or another, but ongoing and unresolved arguing related to how bills get paid, who's responsible for rising debt, and so on is a sign that finances are a source of stress in your relationship. Money-related disputes are the number-one cause of divorce in the U.S.

✔ **Being refused credit:** Something must be seriously wrong if a creditor isn't willing to extend credit, even at an extremely high interest rate.

✔ **Writing bad checks:** Writing bad checks by mistake means you've lost control of your checking account. You need to take immediate steps to remedy the situation.

✔ **Getting calls from multiple creditors:** If you fall behind on one bill, chances are you can handle it yourself. As the number of creditors calling you for late payments grows, the problem becomes exponentially more complex.

✔ **Addictive behavior:** Any addiction can be a problem, including alcohol, drugs, or the Internet. Anything that takes time, energy, and resources away from a paying job and your family (if you're supporting a family) can cause financial problems. Identify addictions early and nip them in the bud.

Understand the Cost of Bad Credit

. . . .

*T*he extra interest you have to pay is only the tip of the bad-credit iceberg. The real cost of bad credit is in reduced opportunities, family stress, and having to associate with lenders who see you as a mark. This section fills you in on some of the unpleasant consequences of bad credit.

✔ **Fees:** Creditors may add fees, such as late fees, over-limit fees, legal fees, repo fees, penalty fees, deficiency payments, and default rates, to your balance. As bad as the fees can be on your credit cards, they can be even worse on your secured loans. If you fall behind in your house payment three months, you can be hit with huge fees to the tune of thousands of dollars.

✔ **Higher interest rates:** The lower your credit score, the higher the interest rate you have to pay; the higher your score, the lower the interest rate. Making matters worse, the policy of *universal default* says that if you have an issue with one lender, all your lenders can hike your rates as well, even though you're still paying the others on time and as agreed. Some companies even use a deteriorated credit score as reason to escalate your rates to the penalty level.

✔ **Less than favorable loan rates:** Shopping around for the best lender becomes even more important when your credit score isn't as attractive as it could be. Lenders may say yes to a loan but at a higher cost. In a time of tight credit, you may not qualify for a loan at all.

✔ **Lost employment opportunities:** Increasingly, credit checks are a standard part of the hiring and even the promotion process at companies large and small throughout the United States. Businesses reason that the way you handle your finances is a reflection of your behavior in other areas of your life.

✔ **Higher insurance premiums:** A strong correlation exists between bad credit and reported insurance claims. Insurance companies run a credit check when determining your premium. What this means is that bad credit costs you a bundle in insurance-premium increases and may result in your insurance being denied.

Get Copies of Your Credit Report and Scores

● ●

*T*hree main sources of credit information dominate the credit industry today: Equifax, Experian, and TransUnion. These credit bureaus are basically huge databases of information from lenders, bill collectors, courts, public utilities, and others who provide goods and services to you today and get paid down the road. Credit-reporting bureaus don't put data in your file; they simply maintain the files that others put the data into.

A *credit score* is an additional component used in most credit reviews. When lenders order your credit report, they also order your credit score. A credit score summarizes your risk of default in a three-digit score that ranges from 300 to 850.

Get Your Credit Report

Check each of your credit reports at least annually. The information changes fairly frequently, and the different reports contain slightly different information. Fortunately, every American is entitled to one free credit report from each of the three bureaus per year. To get your reports, phone, write, or go to the Web site of each credit bureau:

✔ **Equifax:** P.O. Box 740241, Atlanta, GA 30374; phone 800-685-1111; Web site www.equifax.com

✔ **Experian:** P.O. Box 2104, Allen, TX 75013-2104; phone 888-397-3742; Web site www.experian.com

✔ **TransUnion:** 2 Baldwin Place, P.O. Box 1000, Chester, PA 19022; phone 800-888-4213; Web site www.transunion.com

Alternatively, you can go to a central source to get all three reports:

Annual Credit Report Request Service
P.O. Box 105281
Atlanta, GA 30348-5281
Phone 877-322-8228
Web site www.annualcreditreport.com

Get Your Credit Score

You have to request and pay for a copy of your credit score. Not just any credit score will do. You want your *FICO score,* which is the credit score lenders use. You can get your FICO credit score from only two places:

✔ **myFICO:** Phone 800-319-4433; Web site www.myfico.com

✔ **Equifax:** P.O. Box 740241, Atlanta, GA 30374; phone 800-685-1111; Web site www.equifax.com

The other credit-reporting bureaus — Experian and TransUnion — offer credit scores but not the FICO credit score. If you want your FICO score in addition to an Experian or TransUnion credit report, you need to pay for a report and score package from myFICO.

Check Your Credit Report

*W*hen you have your credit report (see Tip #103, "Get Copies of Your Credit Report and Scores"), you're poised to take the necessary steps to clean up the information that's there — removing outdated or inaccurate details, adding positive information, and even increasing your credit score. By doing all this, you can put yourself in a better position to receive credit and earn the most attractive interest rates when you do borrow. Here's what you should look for in particular:

✔ **Make sure your name is spelled correctly and your Social Security number is correct.** With all the data moving through the financial reporting system, a *Jr.* or a *Sr.* can easily drop out or confusion over a *II* or *III* designation can occur.

✔ **Check to see which of your accounts show up on your credit report.** Remember that your credit report may not show all your accounts, because creditors are only required to supply information to one of the three major credit bureaus.

✔ **Look to see whether accounts are showing the activity they ought to.** If you see accounts that are familiar but activity that isn't — such as a late-payment notation when you're certain you've never been late — report that error to the credit bureau.

Also, if you see accounts you don't recognize, it may be a simple mix-up or something more serious, like identity theft. Again, call the bureau and find out.

✔ **Look for accounts from a bank or store with which you've never done business.** This info may have been added to your credit report because of a misspelled name or incorrect Social Security number.

✔ **Identify which accounts are showing negative activity.** Negative activity can include things like missed or late payments.

✔ **Look for any overdraft protection lines of credit.** These lines of credit often outlive the account they're protecting. Closing these lines of credit can be helpful if you have a lot of credit available.

✔ **Check out all the addresses the reports list for you.** Incorrect addresses can lead to incorrect information.

Dispute Inaccurate Info on Your Credit Report

ou can't legally remove accurate and timely information from your credit report — whether it's good or bad. But the law does allow you to request an investigation of any information in your file that you believe is out of date, inaccurate, or incomplete. You won't be charged for this investigation, and you can do it yourself at little or no cost.

Credit bureaus have made the process for disputing and correcting inaccurate information as easy as possible. Your role is to check your reports at least once a year and, if you see information that looks unfamiliar or wrong, file a dispute.

Any financial institution that submits negative information about you to a national credit-reporting agency has to tell you so. This gives you a heads-up to jump on errors earlier than you could under the old laws.

Each of the three credit bureaus has slightly different procedures for consumers to file disputes, but all three allow you to dispute by phone, online, or by mail:

✔ **Equifax:** Call 800-685-1111, and be sure to have your 10-digit credit-report confirmation number (on your report) available. You can also dispute by mail at Equifax Information Services LLC, P.O. Box 740256, Atlanta, GA 30374 (no confirmation number is required on written correspondence) or online at www.equifax.com.

✔ **Experian:** You can dispute by phone at 888-397-3742; online at www.experian.com; or by mail at P.O. Box 2104, Allen, TX 75013-2104.

✔ **TransUnion:** You can dispute any information by phone at 800-916-8800; online at www.transunion.com; or by mail at TransUnion Consumer Solutions, P.O. Box 2000, Chester, PA 19022-2000 (be sure to include your TransUnion file number, available on your TransUnion credit report).

Here's what happens when you dispute information: After the bureau receives a dispute, it contacts the source that provided the data. That source has 30 days in which to respond. If the source can't verify the data within the time allowed, the information must be removed from your report. If, on the other hand, the information is verified, it stays on your report. In either case, you're notified in writing of any actions that occur as a result of your dispute. If you disagree with the findings, you can ask how the investigation was conducted and who was contacted, as well as add a statement to your report saying why you disagree.

Under the Fair Credit Reporting Act (FCRA), both the credit bureau and the organization that provided the information to the credit bureau — such as a bank or credit-card company — have responsibilities for correcting inaccurate or incomplete information in your credit report.

If you're unhappy with the results of your dispute and think you've been treated unfairly or haven't been taken seriously, contact the Federal Trade Commission (FTC). The FTC works to prevent fraudulent, deceptive, and unfair business practices in the marketplace and to provide information to help consumers spot, stop, and avoid them. To file a complaint or to get free information on consumer issues, visit www.ftc.gov or call 877-382-4357 (TTY 866-653-4261).

Be assertive

Being assertive means not giving up until you resolve an issue. It means asking pointed, relevant questions and then asking follow-up questions until you're sure you understand what's going on or the issue has been resolved. It means that you follow up on everything and you push the envelope of your comfort level, and the comfort level of the people with whom you're dealing. If your lender's representative tells you that she'll get back with you in a couple days and she doesn't, call her back and politely say that you haven't heard anything and wanted to follow up. Explain to her that you want to get this matter worked out and behind you, and you don't want to miss any deadlines or cutoff dates.

Add Positive Info to Your Credit Report

∙ ∙

*T*he best way to get positive information inserted into your credit report is to make payments to your creditors on time and in the full amount each month. Do so for a year or more, and you'll have made great strides in improving your credit history and your credit score. You can also add some information to your credit report. Consider doing the following:

✔ Requesting that your good accounts be added to your report if they aren't already showing up

✔ Adding a 100-word statement to explain certain information, such as late payments

✔ Opening new types of credit accounts, such as an installment account if you have only credit cards

Be careful when using this tactic to improve your credit score. You can do more harm than good. If you open an account with a large amount of available credit, it's likely to push your available credit over the limit of what's acceptable by lenders.

Bring Credit Card Debt Under Control

*T*he first thing to do when you need to get your credit card debt under control is to look over each of your credit-card statements each month. You may be surprised to find charges on your account that aren't yours, or you may not have realized just how much you're charging each month. If you see anything you're unsure about or that's incorrect on any part of your credit-card statement, call the credit-card company immediately and resolve the issue. The following sections outline other ways to regain control over your use of credit cards.

Stop Solicitations

By limiting or eliminating credit-card and loan offers, you'll be less apt to apply for this "easy" credit. One way to minimize the number of solicitations you receive from would-be lenders is to get your name added to no-call or no-solicitation lists. Eliminating these solicitations also reduces the number of opportunities identity thieves have to establish credit in your name — and saves a few trees.

✔ Call 888-5OP-TOUT (888-567-8688) to have your name removed from the marketing lists that are sold by credit bureaus to potential lenders.

✔ Write the Direct Marketing Association to be removed from its direct mail and phone lists. Be sure to write a letter to each of the following:

  • Mail Preference Service, P.O. Box 643, Carmel, NY 10512

  • Telephone Preference Service, P.O. Box 1559, Carmel, NY 10512

✔ Contact the Direct Marketing Association online and request that your information be removed from its mail, telephone, and e-mail marketing databases:

  Mailing lists: www.dmachoice.org/MPS/proto1.php

  Phone lists: www.the-dma.org/cgi/offtelephonedave

  E-mail lists: www.dmachoice.org/EMPS

✔ Register for the National Do Not Call list at www.donotcall.gov or by calling 888-382-1222.

Registering your name with no-call or no-solicit lists doesn't in any way affect your ability to borrow money.

Cut the Cards

Identifying the problem is the first step to digging out of debt. The second step is often difficult for hard-core credit card junkies: cut up your credit cards. Yep, pull out the scissors and start snipping.

Some credit providers can't officially close the account until you pay in full, but do not, under any circumstances, use a credit card until you pay your debts in full. If you're deeply in debt, paying it off can take several years. But after you're out from under the burden of excessive debt, the relief you experience more than makes up for the inconvenience of going without credit for a long stretch of time.

Sometimes you need a credit card of some sort for making airline reservations, buying online, or renting a car. If so, get a check card from your bank.

Take Credit Solutions into Your Own Hands

. . . .

*B*y being proactive and acting quickly, you can solve some credit problems on your own. Other problems, because of their magnitude or what you risk losing, require the help of a competent credit counselor (see Tip #109, "Seek Help for Credit Problems" for details on the latter).

The credit situations outlined here are ones that you can probably resolve without much help. If you go it alone, be sure that you identify the cause of the problem and resolve it, know how much money you have to work with, and act quickly.

Missing a Month's Payment on a Credit Card

If you can't make this month's payment or if you've missed a month's payment already on your credit card, be proactive. As long as you know what you can afford, and you don't mind explaining your situation over the phone, you can get quick results. Call the toll-free customer-service number and tell the rep who you are, what happened, and how you want to handle it. If you need a break from having to make payments, say so. If you can make up the missed payments over the next month or two, make an offer (just make sure your offer is something you can make good on).

Usually, if you're proactive and contact credit-card companies before they contact you, you establish yourself as a good customer who needs and deserves special consideration — much better than an elusive customer who's behind in payments, doesn't call, and may be a collection risk.

You may be asked to do more than you think you can. Do *not* agree to anything you don't think you can deliver. Saying that something isn't possible, and explaining why, is much better than caving in but not being able to follow through. Ask to talk to a supervisor — he or she has more authority to bend the rules.

Missing a Mortgage Payment or Paying Late

If you're within the grace period allowed in your loan documents, just send the money in if it will make up the shortfall. If you're past the grace period, you have varying amounts of time to make up the deficit, depending on the state you live in. Suppose you're behind on your monthly payment of $1,000. If you can send only $500 extra with the next month's $1,000 payment, you'll still be short $500, right? Wrong. You may be behind the full $2,000 if the bank doesn't accept either payment because you didn't catch up in full. If you aren't far behind and you can catch up in one shot, do it. Otherwise, get help from a credit-counseling agency.

Deferring Student Loans

Getting a short-term waiver on student loan payments isn't difficult if you have a good reason. Unemployment, a low-paying job, illness, a return to school — each of these reasons may qualify you for a short-term waiver, but only if you give the lender a call before you get into a default situation. The student-loan people are usually very forgiving as long as they think you're playing it straight with them.

Seek Help for These Credit Problems

• •

*C*ertain situations create more financial stress than others. Credit counseling can help with the three main categories of problems that can wreak the most havoc:

- ✔ **Multiple bill collectors:** Most people can handle one or two collectors. But when you get to five, ten, or even more, you're pulled in many directions at once by their conflicting demands. It takes only one unreasonable creditor to make your situation impossible.

- ✔ **Joint credit problems:** Credit problems are exacerbated when you share them with someone who doesn't see things the way you do. Compromising is hard enough in good times; in stressful situations, finding solutions agreeable to everyone can be much more difficult.

- ✔ **Debts that are backed by assets:** If you take out a loan to buy a car, your loan is secured by that car. If you take out a loan to buy a house, your loan is secured by the house. In other words, *security* is what you stand to lose if you don't or can't pay back the money you borrowed. As a general rule, the more security lenders have, the less willing they are to work with you to solve what's clearly "your problem." It's easier than most people think to lose these assets if you're not making payments. If you can't come up with the entire deficit quickly, get help before things snowball.

#110

Work with a Credit Counseling Agency

• •

A credit-counseling agency serves as an objective party to help you sort through your problems, see your situation through the eyes of professional, give you some credit education, offer personalized budgeting advice, and design a customized plan to get you out of debt — all for nothing or next to nothing.

A credit-counseling agency analyzes your sources of income and your expenses. The agency will

- ↙ Detail what you owe.

- ↙ Give you an organized picture of your financial situation.

- ↙ Provide options that match your resources, lifestyle, and goals.

- ↙ Tell you the steps you need to take to reach those goals.

Whether you first contact a credit-counseling agency by phone, e-mail, or in person, the counselor asks you why you're there, what you want to accomplish at the meeting, and what your short-term and long-term goals are.

Then some fairly detailed data-gathering takes place. You're asked about your income sources and tax deductions, as well as your monthly expenses. Having a good idea about what your monthly expenses are helps, but it isn't a requirement — if you don't know, the credit counselor can help you estimate them. A quick subtraction of expenses from income tells you how much you have available for monthly debt service, if any. The counselor will suggest ways to adjust your expenses or income, to get you to a *positive cash-flow* position (in which more money is coming into your household than is going out).

Next, you and the counselor go over all the debts you have to pay. The positive cash flow from the earlier calculation is applied to the amount you have to pay. If anything is left over, you're basically done — you leave with an action plan and a budget you can follow to keep your expenses in line with your income. If the result is negative (you have more expenses than you have income), you and your counselor rework the expenses to free up cash flow and he or she tells you what your debt service would be under a *debt-management plan*.

This process of reducing your expenses and increasing your income continues until you and the counselor get to a positive cash flow or it becomes apparent that, no matter what you do, the numbers just don't work in your favor. If you can't get to a positive cash flow, the counselor refers you to an attorney or other community resources for additional help.

Alas, there is no magic wand to make all your financial problems disappear, but a good certified credit counselor always offers solutions. Expect more than one solution, and expect some solutions you don't like. Your counselor will give you a balanced perspective of what you need to do, how long it will take, and what resources are available to help you along the way. Your counselor will probably discuss bankruptcy, as well as other solutions. The key: The counselor proposes solutions not just in the light of your current situation, but also in light of your future needs.

Beware of services that overcharge and underserve the credit-impaired, offering a product based on technology rather than public-service, mission-oriented values. If you're already up to your eyeballs in debt, avoid these debt mills like the plague! You need the maximum help for the minimum cost and you won't find it with them.

Create a Debt-Management Plan

● ●

*I*f you're in debt crisis or you're concerned you may be getting close to it, a debt-management plan from a good credit-counseling agency may be just the solution. For a small monthly fee the agency handles both communications and payments on your behalf, and it includes revised payments that:

- Are acceptable to all your creditors
- Leave you enough money to handle your living expenses
- Generally get you out of debt in two to five years

When creditors realize that you can't meet the original terms of your credit cards or other loan agreements, they also realize that they're better off working with you through your credit counselor. Under a debt-management plan, your creditors are likely to be open to a number of solutions that are to your advantage. These solutions include:

- Stretching out your payments so that the combination of *principal* (the amount you originally borrowed) and interest will pay off your balance in 60 months or less

✔ Changing your monthly payments to an amount you can afford to pay

✔ Reducing your interest rate and/or any fees associated with your loan

✔ Stopping creditors from hounding you day and night

Sounds like a good deal: lower interest rates, smaller payments, and all. Well, the debt-management plan isn't a free lunch. The minuses may include the following:

✔ A possible negative impact on your credit report (although just being in a debt-management plan doesn't affect your FICO score)

✔ An increase in interest rates (unless you pay in full and through the credit-counseling agency you originally signed up with)

✔ Restricted access to credit during the term of the plan

✔ Difficulty in changing credit-counseling agencies after you begin a debt-management plan

Talk to Creditors to Work Out a Solution

*F*or many people, communication isn't easy. Compound this apparently widespread communication disability with emotion, guilt, and maybe even some anger, and you have a recipe for conflict and communication breakdown. Yet this is the very situation that thousands of people find themselves in when they're trying to put a stop to their credit crises. People just like you pick up the phone, call their creditors, and find themselves in a yelling match with a representative who seems to have the sensitivity of a robot.

Is resolution possible here? Yes — if you do your homework, offer a solution, follow through with what you promise, and follow these steps:

1. **Contact your creditor promptly.**

2. **Explain your situation.**

   Here are some elements you want to communicate (using a phone conversation as an example):

   • Begin the conversation on a positive note.

   • Get the person's name.

- Briefly (in a couple minutes or so) explain your circumstances.

- Stick to the facts.

3. Offer a solution.

Whatever your proposed plan, be sure to cover these bases:

- Offer an estimate of how long you realistically need to rectify the situation.

- Propose a specific payment figure and plan that you can manage.

4. Cover all the bases.

After you agree to terms, ask the creditor to mail or e-mail a letter with the new agreement to you; after all, you want to avoid any misunderstanding. If this letter doesn't seem to be forthcoming from your contact, or if you don't receive written documentation of the new terms in a few days, follow up with the creditor in writing.

Negotiate a Payback Arrangement with Collectors

● ●

*S*uppose you get a call or a letter claiming you have a past-due financial obligation. Even if you're sure you owe the money, asking for details — which account, what the bill was for, the age of the debt, when the statement was mailed to you — never hurts. Why? For two good reasons:

✔ The collector may be wrong.

✔ You may be the victim of a scam.

When you and the collector are in agreement that all the particulars of the debt are legitimate, it's time for you to make an offer to resolve the obligation — whether the cause of the delinquency was an unintended error or unfortunate circumstance.

You want to convey your concern and reassure the collector that you're sincere in your commitment. But that doesn't mean you shouldn't negotiate for an arrangement that favors you. As you're discussing the repayment terms, think of some concessions you want to have. For example, you may want the creditor to

✔ Keep it from the credit bureaus

✔ Waive late fees

✔ Give you a lower interest rate

If you're 90 days or more past due, you're on thinner ice because you're more seriously late and three months of fees will probably be in the $100 vicinity. You may just ask for bureau-reporting forgiveness (that costs the creditor nothing). If, on the other hand, your situation is such that you can't pay back the money right now, you may not have a leg to stand on when it comes to asking for favors. You may just have to set your sights on a reasonable repayment plan that you can live with.

If you're under extreme financial duress, go a step further and ask whether the creditor has a hardship program. You may have to meet some qualifications, but if you do, you could see your interest rate drop dramatically, perhaps even to zero, and have your payments lowered for six months to a year.

Avoid Credit-Repair Scams

• •

*C*redit-repair companies can't do anything legitimate that you can't do for yourself. Some are shady, some aren't, but you have to be on the lookout for scams. Run for cover whenever a credit-repair company

- ✔ Tries to loan you money
- ✔ Plans to sell your name to other lenders
- ✔ Boasts that it can remove truthful information from your credit reports

Sometimes advisors suggest that you apply for credit by using a Social Security number similar to but slightly different from your real number, hoping that instead of matching this fake number with an existing file, the credit bureau will create a new one. Taking this step is both illegal and stupid.

Keep Credit Under Control While Unemployed

Your credit-report experience tends to follow your personal financial experience, so you can do a few things to protect your credit while you're unemployed.

Use Credit during Unemployment

When you find yourself unemployed, if you've established savings (regardless of the amount) and you have some available credit lines, you have two tools that will help you get through this time without damaging your credit. By using a combination of credit and cash, you can put together a new plan that includes finding that new job and implementing a budget that works while you do so.

Stay away from cash advances! Spending money this way costs more than using a credit card. Using your credit card to buy a $10 item may seem silly, but it's better for you than using a $10 cash advance. Cash advances come with an extra fee, often have a higher interest rate, and often have a maximum lower than your credit limit.

Look at credit differently

When you're unemployed, use credit for basic living and job-hunting expenses, preserving your cash for as long as possible by using credit first. This advice is just about the opposite of what most people tell you. But when you use credit for these expenses, you do so for a limited period of time and for a specific, worthy purpose. Think of it as borrowing money for a surefire investment: your future. Keep your overall spending to essentials by closely following a budget (see the next section).

Refigure the family budget

To keep your spending in line with your reduced resources, discuss the situation and the need to temporarily reduce expenses with your family. Don't be embarrassed in front of the kids. This situation is an important lesson in reality, and you can show them how adults face difficult issues and win.

If your severance is being paid out over time or if you haven't yet received it, ask your employer or human resources department to raise your deductions to the maximum allowed: ten. (Don't ask for more than ten, because the IRS wants a report of anyone with more than ten deductions.) This strategy results in more cash now, when you need it.

Yes, you may owe some taxes on this money in April (though your job-hunting expenses and reduced earnings for the year may offset that). You want to maximize today's income at the possible expense of tomorrow's demands.

Protect Your Credit Lines

The downside to using credit for basic living expenses (a sound strategy during unemployment) is that you *may* do some damage to your credit. Here are some tips for protecting your status while leveraging your available credit to get through this challenging time:

- **Keep balances at less than 50 percent of your available credit.** Spread your credit use over several accounts to keep your balance on each card at less than 50 percent. Rather than having, say, a $2,000 balance on one card and a $0 balance on three cards, spread the amount over four cards — with each balance at $500.

- **Make all payments on time.** Thirty-five percent of your credit score has to do with whether you make payments on time.

- **Pay your mortgage first.** Not all bills are created equal — and your mortgage is the most unequal of them all. If you can afford to pay only one bill, pay this one. Partial payments don't work, and falling behind 90 days begins a difficult-to-stop foreclosure process.

Use Home Equity to Consolidate Debts

*I*f you have credit card debt, a second mortgage, or other loans in addition to your first mortgage, debt consolidation can take a chunk out of your monthly expenses, freeing up money to cover other bills.

Discover Debt-Consolidation Options

Consider exploring the following options for consolidating debt:

- Refinance your mortgage.
- Take out a home equity loan.
- Take out a home equity line of credit.

When you're already having trouble paying your bills, you may have damaged credit, which makes obtaining the loan you need to consolidate your debt that much more difficult. If that's the case, look at other means of consolidating, like getting one of these types of loans:

✔ An *unsecured loan* allows you to pay off the old debt and make one monthly payment to the bank.

✔ A *secured loan* requires that you put up some form of collateral so the bank has something it can take from you and sell to cover the debt.

Which is best — a secured or unsecured loan? That depends on your situation. Discuss your options with a qualified loan officer or mortgage broker in your area.

When you borrow money, read and fully understand the documents before signing them. Know what the provisions are, when payments are due, what happens to surplus funds if collateral is sold for more than is required to pay off the loan, and so on. Have an attorney review the document and advise you of any potential issues before you sign.

Compare the Costs of Loans

Consolidating debt with a loan you pay too much for isn't a smart move when your goal is to lower payments and reduce what you owe. You can select from hundreds of loan types, but the bottom line is how much the loan costs in the long run. The best way to compare loans is to determine the total cost of each loan over the life of the loan:

1. **Add up the fees charged to process the loan, including the loan origination fee, points, and closing costs.**

2. **Multiply the monthly payment by the number of months it will take you to pay off the loan in full.**

3. **Add the amounts from Steps 1 and 2 to determine the total cost of the loan.**

4. **Subtract the total amount you expect to pay toward principal over the life of the loan.**

   Ask the bank for an amortization worksheet for each loan to see how much principal you'll have paid at the time you expect to sell the house and pay off the loan.

The result is the total cost of the loan. Simply choose the loan that costs the least over the life of the loan.

Take Control When Foreclosure Looms

• •

*A*s soon as you begin to sense that your financial situation has taken a turn for the worse, you and the rest of your household need to work together to keep the problem from getting worse. Picture yourself in a boat that's taking on water. Before you start bailing out the water, find the holes and plug them.

Freeze Your Finances

When foreclosure strikes, the first order of business is to get a handle on your finances. Do whatever possible to keep more cash flowing in than flowing out — boost income with overtime or a second job, slash unnecessary expenses, and sock away as much money as possible. If you have children, trimming the fat is more stressful, because you may fall into the trap of thinking you're depriving your children or letting them down. Keep in mind that the one thing your kids want and need most is *you,* not the stuff you buy them. These ideas can get you started:

- Instead of ordering Chinese and renting videos, cook a meal and have a family game night.

- Put off that trip to the salon for a manicure, pedicure, facial, or hair appointment. Do it yourself.

- Scale back on this year's vacation; take day trips and pack a picnic lunch.

- Instead of treating your friends and family to dinner, invite them over for a pitch-in.

What you do with added income and savings depends on your strategy. If you're committed to saving your home, set aside the extra cash for reinstating the mortgage or working out a payment plan with the bank. If saving your home is a lost cause, you may decide to squirrel away as much money as possible during the redemption period so that you have a sufficient nest egg to take with you when you move.

Prioritize Your Bills

Part of the process of stabilizing your current situation is prioritizing your bills. So when you're facing foreclosure, pay your bills in this order:

- Property taxes
- Secured debts
- Homeowner's insurance
- Utility and grocery bills
- Unsecured debts

302 Part VI: Staying Afloat If the Boat Starts to Sink _____

Know Who to Contact

Your most valuable assets in foreclosure are people who can assist you, so draw up a list of people you can lean on. Your list may include the following:

- Friends and relatives
- Bank representative
- Real estate agent (*Note:* Selling the home is often the best option in foreclosure cases.)
- Register of deeds
- Sheriff
- Bankruptcy attorney
- Foreclosure attorney

Gather Important Documents

Before you get too far into the foreclosure fight, gather important documents and other materials you'll be called upon to deliver at some point in the process. The most important of these legal documents:

- Mortgage, deed of trust (if you purchased your home through a bank), or contract for deed (if the seller provided financing
- Modifications to the mortgage or promissory note
- Deed
- Correspondence
- Notice of default

- Sheriff's or trustee's deed

- Canceled checks

- Bank statements

- Listing agreement

- Current appraisal

- Phone logs

- Other stuff (Keep anything else you think may be relevant. Having more than you need is better than needing something later and not having it.)

If you can't find a copy of your deed or mortgage or anything else that's part of the public record, schedule a trip to your local county building; you can usually obtain copies of most documents by paying a small per-page copy fee.

Draft a Plan of Attack to Offset Foreclosure

• •

*I*f you're facing possible foreclosure, you need a plan. Are you going to try to save your home? Do you want to sell it to get out from under the burden? Does it make sense to simply live in the home as long as possible and then bail out before the sheriff comes to evict you? Following are some options:

✔ Filing for bankruptcy: This is a costly option. Consult with a reputable bankruptcy attorney in your area before making any final decisions.

✔ Reinstating your mortgage: If you think you'll be unable to pay off the loan in addition to making your mortgage payments, reinstatement may not be the ideal solution for you.

✔ Arranging for a redemption

✔ Haggling for a forbearance: A *forbearance agreement* is similar to reinstating, but you don't have to pay a lump sum all at once.

✔ Negotiating a mortgage modification

✔ Refinancing your home with another lender: Be wary of shady loan originators who may try to take advantage of you by selling you a loan (one with a very high interest rate or an adjustable-rate mortgage [ARM] with a low teaser rate that's likely to rise suddenly) that'll put you in worse shape months or years down the road.

✔ Living off your home with a reverse mortgage.

✔ Selling the house

✔ Deeding the house to your bank in lieu of foreclosure: When offering a deed in lieu of foreclosure, make sure the bank provides you with a formal release of all obligations for repaying the debt. Otherwise, the bank may be able to file for a deficiency judgment if the house sells for less than what you owe on it; you're then responsible for paying the difference.

✔ Selling the house to an investor

✔ Moving out and leaving the keys

When you serve your country in the military, you're eligible for a few well-deserved perks, including mortgage payment relief and foreclosure protection. The Servicemembers Civil Relief Act (SCRA) of 2003 (formerly the Soldiers' and Sailors' Civil Relief Act of 1940) provides this protection for eligible service members. For more information, go to www.hud.gov/offices/hsg/sfh/nsc/qasscra1.cfm.

In deciding how to proceed, weigh your options rationally:

1. **Lay all options on the table, no matter how unrealistic they may seem right now.**

2. **Arrange the options in order, from the ones that sound most attractive to the ones that sound least attractive.**

3. **Move to the bottom any options that are likely to land you back in the same place you are now (or worse).**

4. **Get on the same page as your spouse or partner.**

   The execution of your plan will be most effective if you present a unified front. You both need to get with the program, agree not to fight (too much), and join forces to develop a solid plan and put it into action.

In a slow market, the lender may be more amenable to working with you. After all, the bank stands to lose if nobody in the area can afford its mortgage payments. If the lender is smart, it'll try to work out a solution that enables you to stay in your home and eventually start making payments again.

Understand Types of Bankruptcy

• •

*I*f you're filing for bankruptcy, your basic choice is between a bankruptcy that doesn't involve any type of repayment plan (Chapter 7 bankruptcy) and one that does (Chapter 13). Base your decision on what's best for you and your family, not on what you think will make your creditors happy.

Chapter 7: Straight Bankruptcy

Chapter 7, or *straight bankruptcy,* is the belly-up version that most people envision when they hear the word *bankruptcy.* If you file under Chapter 7, most of your debts are eliminated, and some of your property may go to your creditors. You don't have any repayment plan; your debts simply disappear.

Assets that are *nonexempt* (or ripe for picking by creditors) may be seized and sold by the trustee, with the proceeds distributed to your creditors. In the real world, however, most consumer bankruptcies are *no-asset* cases. In other words, you have nothing for creditors to take, except the shirt on your back and other items that are off-limits. If things work out, you lose only your debt.

To qualify for Chapter 7 bankruptcy, you need to jump these hurdles:

✔ **Can you pass the Means Test?** The Means Test requires a complicated set of calculations that are supposed to identify those consumers who can pay a significant portion of their bills and should be required to do so instead of shedding all their obligations in Chapter 7.

✔ **Are you acting in good faith?** Some judges consider whether you're acting in *good faith*. They may ask whether

- Your bankruptcy was necessitated by sudden illness, calamity, or unemployment.

- You made unnecessary eve-of-bankruptcy purchases far exceeding your ability to pay.

- Your bankruptcy paperwork is complete and accurate.

Chapter 13: Debt Repayment Plans

In filing a Chapter 13 bankruptcy, you propose a debt repayment schedule, and, for the next 36 to 60 months, you pay what you can afford. The two types of payments that you may have to make are

✔ To a trustee, who doles out money to creditors.

✔ So-called *payments outside the plan,* which are payments that come due after you file and are paid directly to the creditor.

Creditors usually receive only a small percentage of what they're owed and typically must settle for pennies on the dollar. After that, you're home-free. Even if you can't *eliminate* debts, you can still use Chapter 13 to keep creditors off your back while you pay them in full over three to five years.

Only individuals with regular income (no corporations, no partnerships) can file under Chapter 13. The source of your income isn't important, provided it's regular and stable. Your income can be wages, self-employment profits, unemployment benefits, or even assistance from friends and family.

Try to Avoid Bankruptcy

∙ ∙

*Y*ou don't need to file bankruptcy to solve a trivial financial problem or when a more targeted remedy is available. Although you shouldn't view bankruptcy as a last-ditch solution, you probably shouldn't make it your first consideration either. If you can get out of trouble without filing, that's wonderful! In fact, you may want to consider the following solutions before deciding that bankruptcy is the way out. If these tips don't do the trick, try the tactics in Tip #121, "Negotiate with Creditors to Avoid Bankruptcy."

Budget

If you can get your financial house in order through discipline and careful budgeting, go for it. The key to realistic budgeting is establishing a reasonable time frame for immediate and long-term goals and adopting a positive attitude that focuses not on what you're giving up but rather on what you're achieving.

Allow Your Family to Bail You Out

If a parent or other family member offers to save your hide, accepting that generosity is tempting. Allowing your family to bail you out may be a wise alternative to bankruptcy, but only if your Guardian Angel

- ✔ Is ready, willing, and able to help.

- ✔ Can pay your debts without suffering financial hardship himself.

- ✔ Can truly solve your problem, not just postpone an inevitable bankruptcy.

Sell Your Assets

If you own assets that you'd lose to a bankruptcy trustee, you may want to consider selling your stuff to pay your debts. If that doesn't raise enough money to pay *all* your debts, it at least helps whittle down your debt load. Consider selling your *nonexempt* assets — those that a creditor can get — not *exempt assets,* those that are off-limits to creditors.

Every state has laws that make certain essential assets exempt or off-limits to creditors, regardless of whether you file bankruptcy. Don't let anyone bully you into selling exempt assets, which in most cases are off-limits even if you don't file for bankruptcy. Most states allow you to keep homesteads up to a specified value, pensions, basic household furnishings, and a modest vehicle.

Transfer Credit-Card Balances

Although trading high interest rates for lower rates is worth checking out, credit-card balance transfers seldom are effective. A *balance transfer* actually is a new loan, with the proceeds going to pay debts that should be pretty far down on your list of priorities. Furthermore, whenever you transfer a balance and then end up in bankruptcy, you may be facing an allegation of fraud, and your creditors may fight to prevent the debts you owe them from being wiped out.

Restructure Home Mortgages

You may be able to free up some cash by restructuring your home mortgage. Basically, you can do this in two ways: arranging a mortgage workout agreement and refinancing.

Taking a home-equity loan doesn't reduce the amount of your mortgage debt. With a home-equity loan, you essentially unbuy your house and then buy it back again. For a variety of reasons, home-equity loans aren't a good idea when you're in financial straits. The most important argument against a home-equity loan is that it creates a lien on your home that survives bankruptcy. Say that after sucking all the equity out of your home to pay your credit-card bills, you still end up in bankruptcy. What you've done is needlessly put your house on the line. The credit-card debts were unsecured and would've probably been eliminated in bankruptcy. But the value of your house secures the home-equity loan. Bottom line: Your home may be the most valuable and important asset that you have, and you're putting it at risk when you play the home-equity credit game.

Negotiate with Creditors to Avoid Bankruptcy

● ●

*A*ttempting a nonbankruptcy solution is worth the effort. If you can find someone who actually has the authority to negotiate, you may be able to cut a deal that works to everyone's satisfaction. You're more likely to succeed if your creditor is a small organization, but if your creditor is a large institution, the task will be more difficult.

Workout Agreements

Traditionally, a nonbankruptcy *workout agreement* — where a debtor reaches a negotiated solution with creditors — falls into one of three categories:

- ✔ Composition arrangements, where all creditors agree to accept less than full settlement of the debts

- ✔ Extension agreements, which merely extend the term for repayment in full

- ✔ Combination agreements, where debts are reduced and paid over an extended time period

The problem with these plans is that all your creditors must go along with it, and so, the more creditors you have, the harder it is to get them to agree. In addition, you'll probably need a lawyer to negotiate settlement agreements, and the legal fees may be exorbitant, if not prohibitive.

Workout agreements are more useful when you have valuable nonexempt assets that are worth enough to pay your debts, but you need some time to sell without having to juggle creditors. In consumer cases, rarely does a debtor have enough assets to pay his debts.

Strange as it may seem, whenever a creditor writes off a debt outside of the bankruptcy context, the amount of the write-off is taxable income to the borrower unless he was insolvent (owed debts exceeding the value of his assets) when the debt was kissed off. If you're in this situation, consider filing Form 982 with your tax return. You can get it on the IRS Web site at www.irs.ustreas.gov/formspubs/index.html (click forms and publications by number).

Threatening Bankruptcy

If you're genuinely considering bankruptcy, unsecured creditors may agree to settle for a pittance simply because when you do actually file, they'd receive nothing.

Assume that you borrowed $50,000 to start a business, which never got off the ground. There's no way you can repay this debt, and all you own is a modest home, mortgaged to the hilt, an old car, and a pension. If you file bankruptcy, the lender won't receive one red cent. If you offer the creditor the money that you'd otherwise spend on filing bankruptcy, about $1,000, he should (if he's thinking rationally) agree to take the money and write off the debt. A thousand dollars is still better than nothing. And you avoid having to file bankruptcy.

The success of this kind of strategy depends on convincing your creditor that you're truly prepared to file bankruptcy. The best way to accomplish that is to hire a well-known bankruptcy specialist to handle the negotiation. That way, the creditor knows that you're serious. But don't ever bluff or threaten bankruptcy unless you're truly prepared to turn in that direction.

Choose Which Bills to Pay When You File for Bankruptcy

• •

*W*hen you can't pay everyone, you need to invest your money where it does the most good or avoids the gravest of problems. Dribbling out money to the most aggressive collectors without an overall plan is a mistake. The payments at the top of your priority list (in order) should be your

- ✔ Rent, or mortgage, if you intend to keep your house
- ✔ Utilities
- ✔ Essential vehicle
- ✔ Fines, if nonpayment would land you in jail
- ✔ Child support and alimony
- ✔ Income taxes
- ✔ Possibly student loans

A note about paying child support and alimony: The consequences for neglecting those obligations are serious, possibly even criminally serious if you're jailed for contempt of court. And many judges have adopted a zero-tolerance approach toward deadbeat parents.

It's no accident that credit cards, loans from finance companies, and medical bills don't make the cut in this list. That's because before creditors in these industries can ever cause you any real trouble they have some hurdles to jump over. Before they can take any of your property, they must sue you and obtain a judgment. Besides, these kinds of debts can be wiped out if you end up in bankruptcy. In addition, if bankruptcy is in your future, you shouldn't repay loans to close friends or family members or loans that these people cosigned for. If you file bankruptcy within one year of making these types of payments, the trustee can get the money back.

Negotiate with the IRS

• •

*T*axpayers and courts long have complained, and with
good reason, about the overbearing presence of the
Internal Revenue Service. A few years ago, however,
Congress passed legislation imposing a wide range of
restrictions on the collection efforts of the IRS. So now,
after years of nurturing its reputation as a bulldog, the
IRS is considerably less arrogant and appreciably more
humble than it once was. And with all the new proce-
dures, IRS collection efforts have become so burdensome
that authorities are more willing to settle than ever
before.

Your Due Process

One of the reforms, known as *collection due process,*
requires the IRS to give you at least 30 days warning
before seizing your property and to notify you of your
right to appeal its determinations.

The appeal provides you with an opportunity to claim
that you're an *innocent spouse* (where your wife or hus-
band fudged a joint tax return without telling you) or
determine the appropriateness of an asset seizure and the
correctness of the amount the IRS claims is due. More
important, you can also propose alternative payment plans
such as *installment agreements* or *offers in compromise*. If

the appeals office turns you down, you can go to federal court and have a judge review the situation. All these new procedural safeguards must take place before any of your property is actually seized.

Negotiate an Installment Agreement

When you owe less than $25,000, getting the IRS to accept a payment proposal is actually pretty easy. An installment agreement requires that you

- Make all payments on time.
- File all future tax returns and pay the taxes due on those returns in full.
- Furnish updated financial information whenever requested.
- Agree that any state or federal refunds be applied to your unpaid taxes.

If you owe $25,000 or more or your request for an installment agreement has been denied, you'll want to hire a lawyer or accountant who's experienced in dealing with the IRS. At this juncture, the IRS can and does insist on detailed information about all your assets and your family's income and living expenses.

Gain "Uncollectible" Status

If the IRS determines that collecting the tax creates an undue hardship, it may suspend collection efforts indefinitely. (In IRS-speak, the account is "53'd," based on the number of the form the revenue officer must complete when reporting that an account is uncollectible.)

Undue hardship means you're unable to meet necessary living expenses if required to make installment payments or if the IRS seizes your assets. The agency distinguishes between undue hardship and *mere inconvenience* — usually finding in favor of the former when it thinks pursuing you isn't worthwhile and finding the latter when going after your assets may be worthwhile. However, even with an undue hardship, your tax isn't abated. Taxes and penalties continue to accrue, and tax liens aren't released. And, of course, the IRS continues to grab your refunds.

Submit an Offer in Compromise

Unlike a payment agreement, an offer in compromise that the IRS accepts actually results in a reduction in the amount you owe. The three grounds for an offer in compromise are

- ✓ Doubt about whether you actually owe the tax.
- ✓ Doubt about whether you have sufficient assets and income to pay the tax in full.
- ✓ Exceptional hardship or unfair or inequitable circumstances caused by payment in-full requirements.

When determining how much it will accept in settlement, the IRS looks at your present assets and future earning ability. It calculates how much it would receive from a quick sale of all your assets and adds a lump-sum amount based on what it figures you'd have been able to pay on taxes during the next 48 months.

Part VII
The Part of Tens

The 5th Wave

By Rich Tennant

"I can always tell when Philip is working on family finances. A 'cursor' appears on both sides of the computer screen."

In this part . . .

You can view reducing what you spend in two ways: as an unpleasant chore that can suck much of the joy out of life, or as an opportunity to evaluate what's really important to you so you can get your spending habits in sync with your values. Here's a little secret: You have a lot more success and fun if you adopt the second perspective.

This part gives you miscellaneous tips on how to cut back on your spending without reducing your quality of living. And because everyone faces financial crises at one time or another, it also delivers advice on how to survive financial emergencies.

Ten Ways to Trim the Money Tree

• •

✔ **Determine which expenses you can eliminate without affecting your quality of life.** For example, can you downgrade your cable and still get the channels that matter most to you?

✔ **Eat out less often.** A family of four can easily spend $30 at a very inexpensive restaurant. You can make that same meal, or a much better one, at home for about one-third of the cost.

✔ **Plant a small vegetable and herb garden.** Not only do you save on grocery bills, but you also benefit from homegrown fun and flavor.

✔ **Cook a giant feast on weekends and freeze the leftovers in individual containers.** Now you have homemade, ready-to-heat meals for a fraction of the cost of quality processed frozen foods.

✔ **Sell items you don't use or need, and purchase quality secondhand items.** Check out Craigslist (www.craigslist.org), an online classifieds site that offers everything from housemates to horseshoes.

✔ **Become a do-it-yourselfer.** If you currently hire someone to mow, clean, or provide other domestic services, explore how much money you could save by doing these projects yourself.

✔ **Get the kids on board.** Involving your children in money management discussions and decisions empowers them to carry out a thrifty lifestyle.

✔ **Donate wisely.** Make a list of charities you *can* donate to and politely decline when you receive a request from the others. Check out Charity Navigator (www.charitynavigator.org), a non-profit organization that rates charities based on their financial health and provides info on how much of your donation actually goes to the programs.

✔ **Revive the dying activity of window shopping.** Gather a group of friends to simply walk through stores, browsing to see what's new and to admire the displays.

✔ **Shop in your own home.** After years of overconsuming, many people have extra dishes, furniture, clothing, and more. When you feel a hankering to redecorate a room or set a special table for the holidays, go shopping through the items you already have.

Ten Ways to Handle Financial Emergencies

· ·

✔ **Plan ahead.** Build a savings cushion of six months of living expenses and make sure you have adequate insurance. Leave room in your monthly budget for surprises. Focus on the plan, and results will follow.

✔ **Pay yourself first.** Put savings away as soon as you get paid. If you can, have it taken from your check and directly deposited into your savings account before you ever see it.

✔ **Reduce tax deductions.** If you get more than $600 a year back in refunds, you'd be better off having that money on a month-to-month basis, earning the interest yourself.

✔ **Earn more money.** Get a second job, work overtime, or ask for that long overdue raise.

✔ **Sell some assets.** Whether you sell your grand piano on eBay or gather your clutter and hold a garage sale, you just may be able to offset some or all of your emergency costs by turning your possessions into ready cash.

- ✔ **Borrow against your home.** If you own a home, have built up equity, and can afford an additional monthly payment, a home-equity line of credit may be just the ticket. Interest payments are incurred only if you draw on the line of credit, and they may be tax deductible.

- ✔ **Borrow from friends and relatives.** Just make sure you put the terms of the loan in writing, establish a regular payment schedule, and pay interest as you would with a traditional loan.

- ✔ **Defer retirement contributions.** If you're regularly contributing to a retirement plan, temporarily funnel the money toward emergency expenses instead.

- ✔ **Seek professional help.** If you see no other way out of your financial crisis, call in the professionals at a credit-counseling agency.

- ✔ **Declare bankruptcy.** Filing for bankruptcy is a legitimate way to handle a financial emergency if nothing else succeeds.

Index

• *F* •

• *N* •

• *O* •

• *P* •

BUSINESS, CAREERS & PERSONAL FINANCE

Accounting For Dummies, 4th Edition*
978-0-470-24600-9

Bookkeeping Workbook For Dummies†
978-0-470-16983-4

Commodities For Dummies
978-0-470-04928-0

Doing Business in China For Dummies
978-0-470-04929-7

E-Mail Marketing For Dummies
978-0-470-19087-6

Job Interviews For Dummies, 3rd Edition*†
978-0-470-17748-8

Personal Finance Workbook For Dummies*†
978-0-470-09933-9

Real Estate License Exams For Dummies
978-0-7645-7623-2

Six Sigma For Dummies
978-0-7645-6798-8

Small Business Kit For Dummies, 2nd Edition*†
978-0-7645-5984-6

Telephone Sales For Dummies
978-0-470-16836-3

BUSINESS PRODUCTIVITY & MICROSOFT OFFICE

Access 2007 For Dummies
978-0-470-03649-5

Excel 2007 For Dummies
978-0-470-03737-9

Office 2007 For Dummies
978-0-470-00923-9

Outlook 2007 For Dummies
978-0-470-03830-7

PowerPoint 2007 For Dummies
978-0-470-04059-1

Project 2007 For Dummies
978-0-470-03651-8

QuickBooks 2008 For Dummies
978-0-470-18470-7

Quicken 2008 For Dummies
978-0-470-17473-9

Salesforce.com For Dummies, 2nd Edition
978-0-470-04893-1

Word 2007 For Dummies
978-0-470-03658-7

EDUCATION, HISTORY, REFERENCE & TEST PREPARATION

African American History For Dummies
978-0-7645-5469-8

Algebra For Dummies
978-0-7645-5325-7

Algebra Workbook For Dummies
978-0-7645-8467-1

Art History For Dummies
978-0-470-09910-0

ASVAB For Dummies, 2nd Edition
978-0-470-10671-6

British Military History For Dummies
978-0-470-03213-8

Calculus For Dummies
978-0-7645-2498-1

Canadian History For Dummies, 2nd Edition
978-0-470-83656-9

Geometry Workbook For Dummies
978-0-471-79940-5

The SAT I For Dummies, 6th Edition
978-0-7645-7193-0

Series 7 Exam For Dummies
978-0-470-09932-2

World History For Dummies
978-0-7645-5242-7

FOOD, HOME, GARDEN, HOBBIES & HOME

Bridge For Dummies, 2nd Edition
978-0-471-92426-5

Coin Collecting For Dummies, 2nd Edition
978-0-470-22275-1

Cooking Basics For Dummies, 3rd Edition
978-0-7645-7206-7

Drawing For Dummies
978-0-7645-5476-6

Etiquette For Dummies, 2nd Edition
978-0-470-10672-3

Gardening Basics For Dummies*†
978-0-470-03749-2

Knitting Patterns For Dummies
978-0-470-04556-5

Living Gluten-Free For Dummies†
978-0-471-77383-2

Painting Do-It-Yourself For Dummies
978-0-470-17533-0

HEALTH, SELF HELP, PARENTING & PETS

Anger Management For Dummies
978-0-470-03715-7

Anxiety & Depression Workbook For Dummies
978-0-7645-9793-0

Dieting For Dummies, 2nd Edition
978-0-7645-4149-0

Dog Training For Dummies, 2nd Edition
978-0-7645-8418-3

Horseback Riding For Dummies
978-0-470-09719-9

Infertility For Dummies†
978-0-470-11518-3

Meditation For Dummies with CD-ROM, 2nd Edition
978-0-471-77774-8

Post-Traumatic Stress Disorder For Dummies
978-0-470-04922-8

Puppies For Dummies, 2nd Edition
978-0-470-03717-1

Thyroid For Dummies, 2nd Edition†
978-0-471-78755-6

Type 1 Diabetes For Dummies*†
978-0-470-17811-9

* Separate Canadian edition also available
† Separate U.K. edition also available

Available wherever books are sold. For more information or to order direct: U.S. customers visit www.dummies.com or call 1-877-762-2974.
U.K. customers visit www.wileyeurope.com or call (0) 1243 843291. Canadian customers visit www.wiley.ca or call 1-800-567-4797.

INTERNET & DIGITAL MEDIA

AdWords For Dummies
978-0-470-15252-2

Blogging For Dummies, 2nd Edition
978-0-470-23017-6

Digital Photography All-in-One Desk Reference For Dummies, 3rd Edition
978-0-470-03743-0

Digital Photography For Dummies, 5th Edition
978-0-7645-9802-9

Digital SLR Cameras & Photography For Dummies, 2nd Edition
978-0-470-14927-0

eBay Business All-in-One Desk Reference For Dummies
978-0-7645-8438-1

eBay For Dummies, 5th Edition*
978-0-470-04529-9

eBay Listings That Sell For Dummies
978-0-471-78912-3

Facebook For Dummies
978-0-470-26273-3

The Internet For Dummies, 11th Edition
978-0-470-12174-0

Investing Online For Dummies, 5th Edition
978-0-7645-8456-5

iPod & iTunes For Dummies, 5th Edition
978-0-470-17474-6

MySpace For Dummies
978-0-470-09529-4

Podcasting For Dummies
978-0-471-74898-4

Search Engine Optimization For Dummies, 2nd Edition
978-0-471-97998-2

Second Life For Dummies
978-0-470-18025-9

Starting an eBay Business For Dummies, 3rd Edition†
978-0-470-14924-9

GRAPHICS, DESIGN & WEB DEVELOPMENT

Adobe Creative Suite 3 Design Premium All-in-One Desk Reference For Dummies
978-0-470-11724-8

Adobe Web Suite CS3 All-in-One Desk Reference For Dummies
978-0-470-12099-6

AutoCAD 2008 For Dummies
978-0-470-11650-0

Building a Web Site For Dummies, 3rd Edition
978-0-470-14928-7

Creating Web Pages All-in-One Desk Reference For Dummies, 3rd Edition
978-0-470-09629-1

Creating Web Pages For Dummies, 8th Edition
978-0-470-08030-6

Dreamweaver CS3 For Dummies
978-0-470-11490-2

Flash CS3 For Dummies
978-0-470-12100-9

Google SketchUp For Dummies
978-0-470-13744-4

InDesign CS3 For Dummies
978-0-470-11865-8

Photoshop CS3 All-in-One Desk Reference For Dummies
978-0-470-11195-6

Photoshop CS3 For Dummies
978-0-470-11193-2

Photoshop Elements 5 For Dummies
978-0-470-09810-3

SolidWorks For Dummies
978-0-7645-9555-4

Visio 2007 For Dummies
978-0-470-08983-5

Web Design For Dummies, 2nd Edition
978-0-471-78117-2

Web Sites Do-It-Yourself For Dummies
978-0-470-16903-2

Web Stores Do-It-Yourself For Dummies
978-0-470-17443-2

LANGUAGES, RELIGION & SPIRITUALITY

Arabic For Dummies
978-0-471-77270-5

Chinese For Dummies, Audio Set
978-0-470-12766-7

French For Dummies
978-0-7645-5193-2

German For Dummies
978-0-7645-5195-6

Hebrew For Dummies
978-0-7645-5489-6

Ingles Para Dummies
978-0-7645-5427-8

Italian For Dummies, Audio Set
978-0-470-09586-7

Italian Verbs For Dummies
978-0-471-77389-4

Japanese For Dummies
978-0-7645-5429-2

Latin For Dummies
978-0-7645-5431-5

Portuguese For Dummies
978-0-471-78738-9

Russian For Dummies
978-0-471-78001-4

Spanish Phrases For Dummies
978-0-7645-7204-3

Spanish For Dummies
978-0-7645-5194-9

Spanish For Dummies, Audio Set
978-0-470-09585-0

The Bible For Dummies
978-0-7645-5296-0

Catholicism For Dummies
978-0-7645-5391-2

The Historical Jesus For Dummies
978-0-470-16785-4

Islam For Dummies
978-0-7645-5503-9

Spirituality For Dummies, 2nd Edition
978-0-470-19142-2

NETWORKING AND PROGRAMMING

ASP.NET 3.5 For Dummies
978-0-470-19592-5

C# 2008 For Dummies
978-0-470-19109-5

Hacking For Dummies, 2nd Edition
978-0-470-05235-8

Home Networking For Dummies, 4th Edition
978-0-470-11806-1

Java For Dummies, 4th Edition
978-0-470-08716-9

Microsoft® SQL Server™ 2008 All-in-One Desk Reference For Dummies
978-0-470-17954-3

Networking All-in-One Desk Reference For Dummies, 2nd Edition
978-0-7645-9939-2

Networking For Dummies, 8th Edition
978-0-470-05620-2

SharePoint 2007 For Dummies
978-0-470-09941-4

Wireless Home Networking For Dummies, 2nd Edition
978-0-471-74940-0

OPERATING SYSTEMS & COMPUTER BASICS

iMac For Dummies, 5th Edition
978-0-7645-8458-9

Laptops For Dummies, 2nd Edition
978-0-470-05432-1

Linux For Dummies, 8th Edition
978-0-470-11649-4

MacBook For Dummies
978-0-470-04859-7

Mac OS X Leopard All-in-One Desk Reference For Dummies
978-0-470-05434-5

Mac OS X Leopard For Dummies
978-0-470-05433-8

Macs For Dummies, 9th Edition
978-0-470-04849-8

PCs For Dummies, 11th Edition
978-0-470-13728-4

Windows® Home Server For Dummies
978-0-470-18592-6

Windows Server 2008 For Dummies
978-0-470-18043-3

Windows Vista All-in-One Desk Reference For Dummies
978-0-471-74941-7

Windows Vista For Dummies
978-0-471-75421-3

Windows Vista Security For Dummies
978-0-470-11805-4

SPORTS, FITNESS & MUSIC

Coaching Hockey For Dummies
978-0-470-83685-9

Coaching Soccer For Dummies
978-0-471-77381-8

Fitness For Dummies, 3rd Edition
978-0-7645-7851-9

Football For Dummies, 3rd Edition
978-0-470-12536-6

GarageBand For Dummies
978-0-7645-7323-1

Golf For Dummies, 3rd Edition
978-0-471-76871-5

Guitar For Dummies, 2nd Edition
978-0-7645-9904-0

Home Recording For Musicians For Dummies, 2nd Edition
978-0-7645-8884-6

iPod & iTunes For Dummies, 5th Edition
978-0-470-17474-6

Music Theory For Dummies
978-0-7645-7838-0

Stretching For Dummies
978-0-470-06741-3

Get smart @ dummies.com®

- Find a full list of Dummies titles
- Look into loads of FREE on-site articles
- Sign up for FREE eTips e-mailed to you weekly
- See what other products carry the Dummies name
- Shop directly from the Dummies bookstore
- Enter to win new prizes every month!

* Separate Canadian edition also available
† Separate U.K. edition also available